CULTURES OF THE WORLD

HONG KONG

Falaq Kagda

MARSHALL CAVENDISH
New York • London

Reference Edition published 1999 by
Marshall Cavendish Corporation
99 White Plains Road
Tarrytown
New York 10591

© Times Editions Pte Ltd 1998

Originated and designed by
Times Books International, an imprint of
Times Editions Pte Ltd

Printed in Singapore

Library of Congress Cataloging-in-Publication Data:
Kagda, Falaq.
    Hong Kong / Falaq Kagda.
      p. cm.—(Cultures Of The World)
    Includes bibliographical references (p.) and index.
    Summary: Surveys the geography, history, government,
economy, and culture of this territory on China's southeastern
coast, made up of a section of the mainland and 235 islands of
various sizes.
    ISBN 0-7614-0692-1 (library binding)
    1. Hong Kong—Juvenile literature. 2. Hong Kong—
Social life and customs—Juvenile literature. [1. Hong Kong.]
I. Title. II. Series.
DS796.H74K34 1998
951.25—dc21   97–15885
                CIP
                AC

INTRODUCTION

HONG KONG'S HISTORY has been characterized by incredible change. Only 150 years ago, it was a rocky, isolated island populated by a handful of farmers. Today, Hong Kong is a bustling hub of business and trade and one of the most densely populated places on earth.

The territory was launched onto the world scene when it became Britain's base for the lucrative Far Eastern trade in tea and opium. Millions of immigrants flooded in, escaping troubles in China and seeking their fortunes. Despite wars, typhoons, overcrowding, and social unrest, the colony thrived.

In 1997, Britain's lease expired and Hong Kong reverted to Chinese rule. This historic event was greeted with mixed feelings by the people of Hong Kong. *Cultures of the World: Hong Kong* explores the challenges facing one of Asia's great metropolises.

CONTENTS

Although the number of people who live on boats is dwindling, the sea still plays an important part in Hong Kong's economy and culture.

CONTENTS

A colorful pagoda at the Temple of Ten Thousand Buddhas.

GEOGRAPHY

HONG KONG IS A TERRITORY of China, situated on China's southeastern coast. It is made up of a section of the mainland and 235 islands of various sizes, with a total land area of 412 square miles (1,067 square km).

To the north, the Sham Chun River forms Hong Kong's border with the rest of China. The Chinese city of Guangzhou (Canton) is around 60 miles (100 km) away, at the mouth of the Zhu Jiang River. Hong Kong is partially situated in the delta of this river. The territory's other close neighbor is Macau, a Portuguese colony, which is located on the opposite side of the Zhu Jiang River delta.

Although Hong Kong has no states or provinces, it can be divided into three main regions based on the territory's geography and history. Hong Kong Island was the site of the original settlement, and it remains the administrative and economic center. Including its nearby islets, it covers 35 square miles (91 square km). The Kowloon peninsula on the mainland and Stonecutters Island, which were the next areas to become part of the territory, cover six square miles (16 square km). The New Territories, made up of a large area on the mainland, Lantau Island, and many smaller islands, has a combined area of 371 square miles (961 square km).

Much of Hong Kong is hilly, and a significant amount of the low-lying terrain is made up of land reclaimed from the sea. Only about 12% of the land is forested, but small tropical and subtropical plants are abundant elsewhere. Hong Kong's small amount of fertile soil is concentrated in the mainland portion of the New Territories, near Deep Bay.

Above: **A peaceful scene along the rocky coastline of Hong Kong Island at Shek O.**

Opposite: **The Central District at night.**

PHYSICAL FEATURES

MOUNTAINS Hong Kong is part of a partially submerged mountain range. A series of ridges runs from northeast to southwest, with the highest mountain, Tai Mo Shan, rising to 3,140 feet (957 m). Other mountains include Lantau Peak (3,064 feet/934 m) and Sunset Peak (2,851 feet/869 m) on Lantau Island, Kowloon Peak (1,978 feet/603 m) on the peninsula, and Victoria Peak (1,818 feet/554 m) and Mount Parker (1,739 feet/531 m) on Hong Kong Island. Many of the mountains are composed of volcanic rocks. On the islands, the steep slopes drop down abruptly to the sea. Some of the small islands are in fact little more than uninhabited, sea-swept rocks.

RIVERS The only river of any size is the Sham Chun River in the north, which forms the border with mainland China. It flows into Deep Bay after collecting a number of small tributaries. Elsewhere in Hong Kong, small streams flow down the sides of the mountain ridges. Reservoirs and catchment systems have reduced the amount of water available downstream.

LOWLANDS Floodplains, river valleys, and reclaimed land occupy less than 20% of the

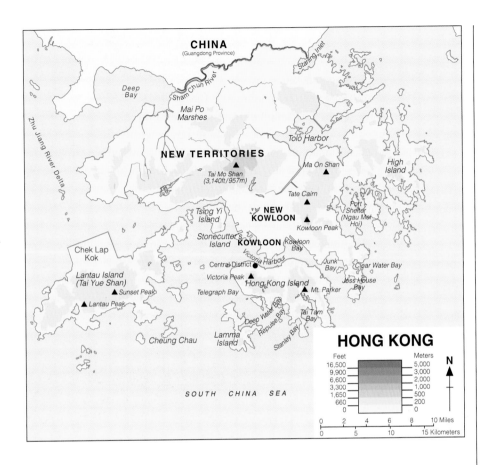

land. The largest lowland areas are in the New Territories, north of Tai Mo Shan. This is where most of Hong Kong's farming occurs. The main urban areas—the Kowloon peninsula and coast of Hong Kong Island—take up only around 10% of the level land. Land is constantly being reclaimed from the sea. In the urban areas, the scarcity of level land has made Hong Kong's real estate prices among the highest in the world.

VICTORIA HARBOR   Hong Kong's spectacular deepwater harbor was the major reason why the British chose the site as their trading base in the 19th century. The harbor is well protected by the mountains on Hong Kong Island. Hong Kong's administrative center, usually known simply as the Central District, lies on the northwest coast of Hong Kong Island. The city of Kowloon lies on the other side of the harbor.

Opposite: **The agricultural land of the New Territories is divided into thousands of tiny farms.**

9

CLIMATE

Hong Kong lies just south of the Tropic of Cancer and has a subtropical climate. Its seasonal changes are well marked, with hot, humid summers and cool, dry winters. The mean annual temperature is 72°F (22.2°C). Daily averages range from 59°F (15°C) in February to 82°F (27.8°C) in July.

During the summer, Hong Kong is buffeted by the monsoon—a moist, warm equatorial wind built up by pressure systems over the Pacific Ocean. The monsoon brings heavy rainfall between May and August, resulting in floods and mudslides. Summer is also the season for typhoons.

In the winter months, pressure builds up over Inner Mongolia, bringing dry, colder winds from the landmass in the west. The dry weather causes water shortages in the cities, forcing Hong Kong to import water from mainland China.

An average of 85 inches (2.16 m) of rain falls in Hong Kong each year. More than half of this falls during the summer months of June, July, and August. Only about 10% of rain falls from November to March.

TYPHOONS

Typhoons (also known as tropical cyclones or hurricanes) generally occur in Hong Kong between July and October. About five or six typhoons affect Hong Kong each year. The torrential downpours and strong winds that usually accompany typhoons sometimes cause great destruction to life and property in Hong Kong. Some of the most destructive typhoons to hit Hong Kong were Wanda (1962), Ellen (1983), Wayne (1986), and Brenda (1989).

When Hong Kong was less developed, major typhoons inevitably resulted in thousands of casualties. Today, improved building design and housing have provided better shelter, and there are fewer casualties. Fishing communities are protected by typhoon shelters, such as the one at Aberdeen (*above*). However, the economic loss caused by typhoons is immeasurable. For example, when a typhoon warning is issued, traffic becomes even more chaotic than usual. Commuting becomes impossible and valuable productive hours are lost. Hong Kong's observatory works closely with the major transportation operators and other government departments to ensure a state of preparedness in the event of a typhoon warning

Despite their adverse effects, typhoons have a positive side. Their rain contributes to the water supply in Hong Kong. They also provide relief from the oppressive heat of a long summer and a welcome day of rest to everyone except meteorologists and emergency service workers.

Hong Kong's only tea plantation, the Lantau Tea Gardens, is found on Lantau. The Hong Kong tea known as Wan Mo Cha ("tea of cloud and mist") comes from this plantation.

ISLAND ATTRACTIONS

LANTAU ISLAND (*above*), also known as Tai Yue Shan, is nearly double the size of Hong Kong Island, but with almost a million fewer residents, it's as peaceful as Hong Kong is hurried. However, recent years have seen the development of new housing and leisure facilities on Lantau Island. The largest settlement is Tai O.

Lantau's main attraction is the Po Lin (Precious Lotus) Monastery, with its beautiful Buddhist temple. The monastery was established by monks from China in the 1950s. In 1991, the Po Lin monks completed construction of the largest statue of Buddha in Asia. It weighs 250 tons (254 metric tonnes) and stands 87 feet (26.5 m) tall.

CHEUNG CHAU has an almost Mediterranean air to it. Two intriguing old temples attract tourists, but locals go there just to walk its streets, where cars are banned. The island is also known for its excellent seafood restaurants. Although densely populated, Cheung Chau has such a relaxed atmosphere that it seems less crowded than it is. At the southern end of the island is a cave that was used by the notorious local pirate, Cheung Po Tsai. Every May, Cheung Chau is host to the famous Bun Festival.

FLORA

Many tropical and temperate species of flora are found in Hong Kong. Most the land area is covered with leafy tropical plants, including mangrove and other swamp plants. The Hong Kong Herbarium, founded in 1878, has about 35,000 specimens, including almost 2,000 known indigenous species and varieties.

After centuries of cutting, burning, and exposure, only 12% of the land is forested. The most common trees are pines, such as the native South China red pine and the slash pine, introduced from Australia. Most of Hong Kong's forest cover, which includes eucalyptus, banyan, casuarina, and palm trees, is the result of afforestation programs since World War II. Forestry plantations within water catchment areas, country parks, and special areas are managed by the Agriculture and Fisheries Department. Fruit trees, including longan, lychee, and starfruit, are abundant in the New Territories.

Some of the oldest areas of woodlands are the *fung shui* ("fung soy") woods, or "sacred groves," found near villages in the New Territories. Believing that the trees improve the spiritual and luck-bringing qualities of the environment, villagers have protected these forests.

Brilliantly colored insects are common in Hong Kong. The territory boasts 200 species of butterflies, and there are over 90 recorded species of dragonflies.

FAUNA

TERRESTRIAL MAMMALS Due to urbanization and disruption of the countryside, wild mammals are rapidly disappearing from Hong Kong. Occasionally, civets, foxes, Chinese leopard cats, and Chinese porcupines may be seen in the New Territories. Leopards and tigers have not been seen for many years. The Barking Deer, a small deer that barks like a dog at night, is now heard only infrequently in wooded areas, and seen even less frequently. Rhesus macaques (a type of monkey), long-tailed macaques, and squirrels can also be found in wooded areas.

BIRDS The Hong Kong Bird Watching Society lists 431 species of birds that have been recorded in an apparently wild state during the past 50 years. The Yim Tso Ha bird sanctuary, near Starling Inlet, provides a home for herons and egrets. The Mai Po Marshes, an area of mudflats, mangroves, and shrimp ponds in the north, are the richest habitat for birds in Hong Kong.

AQUATIC LIFE Hong Kong has a very diverse marine life. There are an estimated 1,800 species of fish in the South China Sea. Clupeoids, croakers, and sea bream are frequently found around Hong Kong. Corals, shelled mollusks, crustaceans, and cephalopods are also common. Marine mammals, including the Chinese white dolphin, the black finless porpoise, the bottle-nose dolphin, and the common dolphin, are protected under Hong Kong's Wild Animals Protection Ordinance.

SNAKES Hong Kong has its share of poisonous snakes, including kraits, coral snakes, cobras, and vipers, but most snakes in Hong Kong are harmless.

Daring monkeys venture out around the Kowloon reservoirs, hoping to pick up scraps of food from picnickers.

ENVIRONMENTAL PROBLEMS

Hong Kong's environment has suffered the consequences of the territory's rapid development. Black smoke billows from power plants, and factories dump chemical wastes into Hong Kong's waters. Boat dwellers throw their garbage directly into the harbor.

As a result, Hong Kong has serious problems with air, land, and water pollution. Pollution has wiped out the schools of fish that used to swim near the main islands, forcing fishing boats to venture farther from shore in search of their catch. The government has introduced envrionmental protection laws in an attempt to clean up the environment.

Trash washed up on a beach on Lamma Island.

15

CITIES, NEW TOWNS, VILLAGES

CENTRAL DISTRICT The city of Victoria on the northwest coast of Hong Kong Island, formerly the capital of Hong Kong, is always referred to by Hong Kongers as the Central District, or simply "Central." This area has been the center of administrative and economic activities in the territory since the British settled there in 1841.

Central's dramatic skyscrapers, colonial buildings, and streets lined with shops are constructed on a strip of land along the coast and on the foothills of the mountains behind. The stunning view of Victoria Harbor, the city, and the mountains has been immortalized in paintings and photographs.

KOWLOON On the other side of the harbor is the Kowloon peninsula, which has undergone massive development in the recent years. Hong Kong's Kai Tak Airport is located on the eastern fringe of the peninsula. Tsim Sha Tsui, on the tip of the peninsula, is a bustling shopping and nightlife district. Factories, businesses, apartment blocks, shops, and markets compete for space. As the peninsula becomes more and more crowded, the urban area is spreading northward into the New Kowloon area.

NEW TOWNS   As a result of housing pressures on Hong Kong Island and the Kowloon peninsula, a number of new towns have been built in the New Territories. These include Tsuen Wan, Tuen Mun, Sha Tin, Tai Po, Fanling, and Yuen Long. Over one quarter of Hong Kong's population now live in the New Territories, and over three-quarters of these live in the new towns. The high density, high-rise apartments are supported by shops, schools, transportation systems, and other services.

SMALL TOWNS AND VILLAGES   An older style of living can still be seen in Hong Kong's villages and small towns. Most of the villages follow the alignment of the river valleys in the New Territories.

Opposite: **A bustling street in Kowloon.**

Below: **A walled village in the New Territories.**

HISTORY

HONG KONG'S HISTORY HAS been shaped by two giants—Britain and China. Until the 19th century, Hong Kong was nothing more than a rocky, sparsely inhabited island off the coast of China. Its modern history began when the British established a settlement on Hong Kong Island in order to conduct trade with China. Hong Kong Island—and subsequently Kowloon and the New Territories—became a British colony.

Hong Kong's growth in the 19th and 20th centuries was dramatic. People flooded into the colony, lured by economic opportunities or fleeing from troubles in their homeland. Despite the interruptions of war and occupation, Hong Kong thrived.

Today, Hong Kong is unique—neither purely British nor purely Chinese. It entered a new era in July 1997, when the British lease of the New Territories expired and Hong Kong reverted to Chinese rule.

During the Ming dynasty (1368-1644), Hong Kong shipped incense to the Yangtze Valley area—hence the name of the island, which means "fragrant harbor."

Left: **In the 19th century, Hong Kong's harbor was visited by junks (Chinese sailboats) and British vessels. Today, junks are a symbol of the old Hong Kong.**

Opposite: **The clock tower in Tsim Sha Tsui, built in 1909, is a legacy of Hong Kong's colonial era.**

19

A lime kiln in Hong Kong. During the Tang Dynasty, lime was used for caulking wooden boats, waterproofing containers, dressing acidic soil, building, and salt production.

ANCIENT HISTORY

Two Neolithic cultures are believed to have inhabited the area around Hong Kong from the fourth millennium B.C. Stone tools, pottery, ornaments, and other artifacts have been unearthed in coastal deposits, suggesting that the ancient inhabitants of Hong Kong depended on the sea for their survival. There is also some evidence of inland settlement. Bronze Age artifacts, including swords, arrowheads, axes, and fishhooks, have also been found. There is evidence, in the form of stone moulds, that metal was worked locally.

Ancient Chinese literary records refer to maritime people known as Yue, who occupied China's southeastern coast. This region was conquered by the Han Chinese from northern China during the Qin (221–206 B.C.) and Han (206 B.C. – A.D. 220) dynasties. Many excavations have turned up coins of the Qin and Han periods. Probably the most outstanding find from this period is the fine brick tomb uncovered at Lei Cheng Uk in Kowloon in 1955, with its array of typical Han tomb furniture.

Archeological finds from later historical periods are rare. The dome-shaped lime kilns that dot the territory's beaches give an insight into one aspect of life during the Tang Dynasty (618–907), when lime was an important commodity.

The first major migration from the north occurred during the Song dynasty (960–1279). However, Hong Kong remained sparsely populated until the 19th century. Its coves and islets were ideal hideouts for pirates of the South China Sea.

BRITISH TRADE WITH CHINA

In 1553, Portugal established a trading base at Macau, about 40 miles (64 km) from Hong Kong. Macau became the principal port for international trade with China and Japan.

British merchants began trading with China from the late 1700s. Tea imported from Asia had become the favorite drink in England, and the tea trade was extremely profitable. However, in line with their policy of isolation, the Chinese authorities imposed severe restrictions on the British merchants. They reluctantly allowed a few British merchants to set up offices in the Chinese port of Guangzhou (Canton), but they dictated the terms of all transactions. They would accept only silver and gold in exchange for their tea.

The British soon found a new product to tempt the Chinese—opium, a powerful narcotic made from the poppy flower. The practice of smoking opium was introduced to China in the 1600s by European sailors. British merchants shipped opium from India to China and received gold and silver in payment. By the late 1700s, it is estimated that China had two million addicts, and the number was growing. Drug addiction and the drain on China's wealth was weakening the country. In 1799, the Chinese declared the opium trade illegal.

In order to get around the trade restrictions imposed by the Chinese, British merchants began looking for a base on which to establish their own trading center. They got their chance in the early 1800s with the outbreak of the Opium Wars.

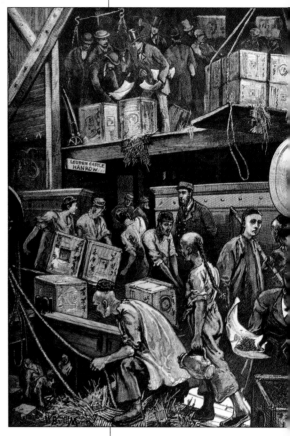

Tea from China is unloaded at the London docks.

21

A sea battle between Chinese and British forces. The Opium Wars ended the long Chinese isolation from other civilizations.

THE OPIUM WARS

In 1839, Lin Zexu, a Chinese imperial commissioner, was sent to Guangzhou to suppress the smuggling of opium into China by British merchants. Lin surrounded the foreign offices with troops, stopped food supplies, and refused to let anyone leave until all stocks of opium had been surrendered. After a siege of six weeks, Captain Charles Elliot, the British government trade representative, authorized the surrender of 20,283 chests of opium.

This enraged the British merchants. They demanded either a commercial treaty that would put trade relations on a satisfactory footing, or the cession of a small island where the British could live under their own flag, free from threats. Hostilities came to a head when a Chinese man was killed in a drunken brawl between British sailors and Chinese fishermen. The British were driven out of China; most escaped to the island of Hong Kong. Soon shooting broke out between the British and Chinese naval forces along the coast. This was the beginning of the First Opium War.

Britain scored an easy military victory. China was forced to open a number of Chinese ports to British trade and residence, cede Hong Kong to Britain, and grant Britain the right to try British citizens in China in British courts. The other European powers soon received similar privileges.

When the British established their settlement in Hong Kong, it was still a rural backwater. The area had 20 villages and hamlets housing a population of about 4,000. Around 2,000 fishers lived on boats in the harbor. Hong Kong possessed only two natural assets—a sheltered deepwater harbor and a strategically location on the trade routes of the Far East.

Merchants' offices and warehouses line the Hong Kong waterfront during the late 19th century.

The Second Opium War resulted from China's continuing objections to the opium trade and from disputes over the interpretation of the earlier treaties. A joint offensive by Britain and France resulted in another defeat for China. The Treaty of Tianjin (Tientsin) was signed in 1858, but the Chinese authorities refused to ratify it. Hostilities resumed, and Beijing (Peking) was captured by the Western allies.

In 1860, China agreed to a treaty that opened 11 more ports, allowed foreign envoys to reside in Beijing, permitted foreigners to travel in the Chinese interior, and legalized the importation of opium. Kowloon was ceded to Britain. Other European countries and Japan also demanded concessions from China. For China, defeated twice, the Opium Wars were the beginning of a century of humiliation by foreign powers.

Chinese refugees line up for water in 1933. During the 1930s, hundreds of thousands of refugees fled the war with Japan and made their way to Hong Kong, bringing Hong Kong's population at the outbreak of World War II to an estimated 1.6 million. At the height of the influx, about 500,000 people were sleeping in the streets.

GROWTH OF THE COLONY

After China's defeat in the First Sino-Japanese War (1894–95), Britain demanded control of the land around Hong Kong for defense purposes. On June 9, 1898, the New Territories—the area north of the Kowloon peninsula up to the Sham Chun River, plus 233 islands—was leased to Britain for 99 years. There was some opposition when the British took over the New Territories, but this soon subsided.

The new settlement in Hong Kong faced severe stumbling blocks at first. Fever and typhoons threatened life and property. Crime was rampant. The population rose from 32,983 (31,463 Chinese) in 1851 to 878,947 (859,425 Chinese) in 1931. After the overthrow of the Qing Dynasty in 1911, many of those fleeing the troubles in China found shelter in Hong Kong. The Chinese influx was unexpected; it had not been anticipated that they would choose to live under a foreign flag.

Despite the colony's uneasy start, the settlement thrived under British rule. Hong Kong became a center of trade with Chinese communities abroad. The late 19th and early 20th centuries were marked by growth and development in education, health, and social services.

At the end of World War I, strong nationalist and anti-foreign sentiments were aroused when German concessions in Shantung (Shandong) were not returned to China. The unrest spread to Hong Kong, resulting in a general strike in 1925–26. With the largest foreign stake in China, Britain was the main target of anti-foreign sentiment. But that was soon to change.

In 1931, Japan occupied Manchuria and tried to take over China's northern provinces. Open war broke out in 1937. This was the beginning of the Second Sino-Japanese War. Guangzhou fell to the Japanese in 1938, resulting in a mass flight of refugees to Hong Kong.

WORLD WAR II

Japan entered World War II on December 7, 1941, when its aircraft bombed US warships at Pearl Harbor. At approximately the same time, Japanese aircraft bombed Kowloon and troops invaded Hong Kong from the Chinese mainland. The Japanese attack forced the British to withdraw from the New Territories and Kowloon to Hong Kong Island. After a week of dogged resistance, the defenders on the island were overwhelmed, and Hong Kong surrendered on Christmas Day.

The three years and eight months of Japanese occupation were terrible years for Hong Kong. Trade virtually ceased, currency lost its value, the food supply was disrupted, and government services and public utilities were seriously impaired. Many residents fled to China and Macau. Towards the latter part of the occupation, the Japanese attempted to alleviate the food problems by organizing mass deportations.

Soon after the Japanese surrender in August 14, 1945, a provisional government was set up by the Colonial Secretary. On August 30, Rear Admiral Sir Cecil Harcourt arrived to establish a temporary military government. Civil government was formally restored on May 1, 1946, when Sir Mark Young resumed his interrupted governorship.

A World War II veteran visits the war memorial in the Central District.

Vietnamese boat people added to Hong Kong's population during the 1970s.

POPULATION GROWTH AND SOCIAL UNREST

With Hong Kong back under British rule, those who has fled Hong Kong during the war returned. The population, which by August 1945 had dwindled to about 600,000, swelled to 1.8 million by the end of 1947.

In 1948–49, as the forces of the Chinese Nationalist government faced defeat in the civil war with the Communists, hundreds of thousands of people entered the territory. By 1950, the population count was an estimated 2.2 million.

The 1960s were a time of mounting tension in Hong Kong. Social unrest and discontent over poor working conditions began to spread. In 1967, severe riots broke out following a labor dispute at a factory. This turned into violent political demonstrations inspired by the Cultural Revolution in China. The disruption affected all aspects of life and temporarily paralysed the economy. But by the year's end, the disturbances were contained and the community continued its tradition of peaceful progress, with notably improved labor conditions enforced by legislation.

RETURN TO CHINA

As the British lease of the New Territories neared its 1997 expiration, concern grew about the future of the territory. Formal negotiations between Britain and China commenced in 1982, when the prime minister, Margaret Thatcher, visited Beijing. In 1984, a Sino-British Joint Declaration was signed by the heads of both governments. The agreement stipulated that all of Hong Kong would be returned to China on July 1, 1997. The Chinese government agreed to establish a self-governing Special Administrative Region under its central government. According to the terms of the Joint Declaration, the current social and economic systems will remain unchanged for 50 years—that is, until 2047.

Signs like these started appearing in Hong Kong in the years leading up to the reversion to Chinese rule.

GOVERNMENT

THE GOVERNMENT OF HONG KONG is currently experiencing a period of great upheaval. Until June 30, 1997, Hong Kong was a colony of the United Kingdom. A governor nominated in London served as the representative of Queen Elizabeth II. An Executive Council and Legislative Council, which were also nominated rather than elected, decided matters of policy and controlled expenditure.

Above: **Police officers on duty.**

Opposite: **A pro-democracy rally in Hong Kong. The protesters are demanding the release of political prisoners in China.**

On July 1, 1997, when the lease of the New Territories expired, Hong Kong reverted to Chinese rule. Under the terms of the Sino-British Joint Declaration on the question of Hong Kong, which was signed in 1984, Hong Kong is now a Special Administrative Region (SAR) of China. Although it is part of the communist People's Republic of China, the SAR's administration retains many features of the colonial system. Democratic reforms that were introduced by the British in the 1980s and 1990s have also left their mark on the SAR government.

The transition from British to Chinese rule has raised many questions in the minds of Hong Kongers. Issues of self-determination, democracy, nationalism, and cultural identity have been hotly debated, and the tensions have sometimes erupted into angry protests. Some Hong Kong residents greeted the reversion to China with patriotic enthusiasm, while others are apprehensive about the social and economic changes that may occur. Some Hong Kongers rushed to obtain British passports so that they will be able to leave if they don't like living in the new Hong Kong. Others emigrated to Britain, the United States, Canada, Australia, and other countries. It is still early for the SAR, and no one can say for sure how events will develop.

THE COLONIAL GOVERNMENT

The current government of Hong Kong is based on the former colonial system. As a British colony, Hong Kong was administered by the Hong Kong government, which was headed by the governor, the representative of Queen Elizabeth II. An Executive Council offered advice to the governor on important matters of policy. A Legislative Council (known as LegCo) passed laws, controlled public expenditure, and monitored the performance of the government. Two municipal councils (the Urban Council and the Regional Council) provided public health, cultural, and recreational services, and 18 district boards provided a forum for public consultation.

Until 1985, the governor was appointed from England, the Executive Council was appointed by the governor, and the members of LegCo were selected by the government. There were no democratic elections. Thus, power was concentrated in the hands of a business and political elite, many of whom were expatriates. It was often said that the Hong Kong had a *laissez faire* ("LESS-ay FAIR") government, meaning that government intervention in economic matters was minimal. Most Hong Kongers were happy to get on with business and not worry about politics.

THE PEOPLE'S REPUBLIC OF CHINA

Across the border, in mainland China, a very different system was operating. The People's Republic of China (PRC) is a communist republic. One party—the Chinese Communist Party (CCP)—controls all major

Above: **Symbols of British rule, once common in Hong Kong, are now being removed.**

Opposite: **The Legislative Council building.**

governmental institutions. Although China has a legislative body, the National People's Congress, real power lies in the hands of the CCP and the State Council, which is the top executive government organ.

When the CCP came to power in China in 1949, they instituted a communist economic system with central planning, state-run industries, and collectivized agriculture. In an effort to abolish the old social and economic systems, private enterprise and religion were banned. The centralized control of the economy ran counter to Hong Kong's system, which was built on free enterprise and minimal government involvement in trade and industry.

In the 1970s, the Chinese government began to introduce economic reforms and encourage foreign investment and trade. However, China continues to be criticized for its repression of dissidents and its unwillingness to adopt democratic reforms.

For much of Hong Kong's history, the Chinese and British governments tolerated each other and benefited from cross-border trade, even during times of political tension. However, the different styles of government, particularly in their approach to economic affairs, became a major issue in the 1980s and 1990s.

Hong Kong residents gather to commemorate the anniversary of the Tiananmen Square massacre.

THE TRANSITIONAL PHASE

When Britain and China began negotiating the terms of Hong Kong's reversion to China in the early 1980s, Hong Kongers were made painfully aware of how little say they had in the running of the territory. Many people felt that Hong Kong was being passed from one master to another without any input from the people who lived there.

In response to calls for greater participation, the Sino-British Joint Declaration stated that the Legislative Council of the SAR would be elected, but the details of this system were not specified. The first elections for the legislature were held in 1985, but only for a minority of seats. Although the Chinese government was unsympathetic toward these belated democratic reforms, the transition seemed to be progressing smoothly.

Meanwhile, the Chinese government prepared the Basic Law that would be the mini-constitution of the SAR. The Basic Law was released on April 4, 1990, in the wake of the Tiananmen Square massacre. It would come into effect on July 1, 1997. The Basic Law made it clear that there would be no territory-wide, freely-held elections for all seats. Only one-third of the Legislative Council would be directly elected.

Despite the apprehension that this caused among Hong Kongers, democratic reforms were proceeding in the colony. Political parties were formed and an election was held in 1991. Pro-democracy candidates won virtually all of the directly elected seats. A new governor, Christopher Patten, was appointed in 1992. Patten increased the power of the Legislative Council and introduced other political reforms, despite objections from Beijing. In response, the Chinese authorities announced that they would dissolve LegCo in July 1997 and replace it with a provisional Legislative Council.

In March 1993, the Chinese government announced the members of a Preliminary Working Committee—a shadow government made up of prominent PRC and Hong Kong political, judicial, and professional figures. As July 1997 drew closer and people accepted the inevitable reversion to China, support for Patten and his reforms declined.

Christopher Patten, the last British governor of Hong Kong.

THE TIANANMEN SQUARE MASSACRE

The political atmosphere in Hong Kong changed suddenly on June 4, 1989, when thousands of people protesting in Tiananmen Square in Beijing, China, were killed, injured, or imprisoned by government soldiers. The Tiananmen Square massacre, as it became known, caused a furor in Hong Kong. Hundreds of thousands of Hong Kongers filled the streets in protest. Many Hong Kongers supported the dissidents in China, sending money or helping them to escape from China. Hong Kongers feared that freedom of speech and other rights would be lost when China took control of the territory. It was in this turbulent atmosphere that the Basic Law was completed.

ONE COUNTRY, TWO SYSTEMS

The principle of the Special Administrative Region is summed up in the phrase, "one country, two systems." According to the Sino-British agreement, the socialist system and policies of the PRC will not be practiced in Hong Kong for the next 50 years. A public education program (*above*) has kept people informed about the transition.

The main elements of the agreement are as follows:

- The existing economic and social systems will continue.
- Free movement of goods and capital, and Hong Kong's status as a free port and separate customs territory, will be ensured.
- Hong Kong will continue to determine its own monetary and financial policies.
- No taxes will be paid to China.
- The Hong Kong dollar will continue to be freely convertible.
- Property rights and foreign investment will be protected.
- The British common law system will be retained, and fundamental human rights will be protected by law.
- The judiciary will remain independent.

THE SPECIAL ADMINISTRATIVE REGION

In 1996, Tung Chee Hwa was chosen to become Chief Executive of the Special Administrative Region. Tung, a shipping magnate, had served as a consultant to both the Hong Kong and PRC governments and was considered diplomatic and politically neutral. The Chief Executive is the leader of the Hong Kong government and is appointed by the PRC government in Beijing. The Basic Law leaves the way open for the Chief Executive to be elected in future.

Under the plans outlined during the transition period, the Chief Executive will appoint the Executive Council, the Administration Secretary, the Financial Secretary, and the Secretary of Justice. The Legislative Council will have 60 members. Twenty of these will be directly elected. This figure will increase to 24 and then 30 over the next decade. The Legislative Council will continue to oversee the day-to-day running of Hong Kong, while defense and foreign affairs will be handled by the State Council in Beijing. Delegates from Hong Kong have been included in the National People's Congress, and this representation is likely to increase.

It is unlikely that the Chinese government will introduce further democratic reforms. Both the Chinese government and the Hong Kong elite prefer to retain a system similar to that of the colonial era—a system based on consultation rather than democratic consent.

Tung Chee Hwa, the Chief Executive of Hong Kong.

ECONOMY

HONG KONG IS ADVANCED in manufacturing, trade, and shipping. It is also a regional financial center and an agent in China's pursuit of modernization. Sustained government policies of free enterprise, free trade, and low taxation have led to the establishment of competitive light industries and an increasingly sophisticated commercial, financial, and transportation infrastructure.

During the 1980s, as Hong Kong's reversion to Chinese rule drew closer, the commercial community was apprehensive about how Hong Kong's free-market economy would mesh with China's centralized system. Multinational corporations wondered whether they should pull out of Hong Kong and relocate elsewhere in Asia. China put most fears to rest, however, by announcing that Hong Kong's economic system will remain intact for the next 50 years.

Opposite: **The container terminal at Kwai Chung near Tsuen Wan. Transshipment is an important part of Hong Kong's economy.**

Left: **Boatbuilders at work in Aberdeen.**

An oil terminal and power station on the island of Tsing Yi.

A LACK OF RESOURCES

Hong Kong is dependent on imports for virtually all of its requirements, including food, raw materials, consumer goods, capital goods, and fuel. Even water is in short supply. Despite Hong Kong's many reservoirs, an increasing proportion of water consumed by the territory is imported from mainland China.

The territory has no mineral resources to speak of. The mining of graphite and lead at Cham Sham (or Needle Hill) and iron ore at Ma On Shan ceased years ago. Small quantities of feldspar and kaolin clay are produced for domestic consumption.

There is no commercial timber felled from Hong Kong's sparse forest cover, and no potential for hydroelectric power from its small streams.

AGRICULTURE AND FISHING

Agriculture in Hong Kong is minimal, since only about 7% of Hong Kong's land area is arable. Of the arable land, about 40% is abandoned or fallow. Only 3% of the population are farmers. Rice cultivation has been replaced by intensive vegetable and pond fish farming, which provide a much greater return on investment. Minimal production of fruits, flowers, sweet potatoes, taro, yam, and sugarcane can still be found.

Marine fishing is conducted in the waters around Hong Kong. Two percent of the land is under fishponds, and a marine fish culture industry is developing in the eastern New Territories.

Next page: **Hong Kong is a major hub of air and sea transportation in Asia.**

Below: **In a village, lemons are laid out in the sun to dry.**

TRADE AND TOURISM

Hong Kong is one of the world's great trade centers, due mainly to the fact that there is no tariff on imports, except for certain luxury goods such as perfumes, cars, gasoline, alcohol, and tobacco.

Almost half of Hong Kong's trade activity consists of imports, generally raw materials and other products for its industries. Also imported are clothing, food, machinery, and other consumer goods. Most imports come from China and Japan. Other major suppliers include the United States, Taiwan, Singapore, the United Kingdom, South Korea, and Germany.

The United States is Hong Kong's main market for exports. Other major markets include China, the United Kingdom, Germany, Japan, and Canada. Re-exports—goods that are imported from one country and immediately exported to another—make up a major portion of the goods shipped from Hong Kong.

Hong Kong is also a major tourist site, with almost nine million visitors passing through each year. Hong Kong has become a popular site for international conferences and exhibitions, and almost a third of its visitors are business travelers. Tourism contributes significantly to the territory's foreign exchange earnings.

TRANSPORTATION

Because of the limited roads relative to Hong Kong's population, the government imposes strict limitations on car ownership. The result is that car ownership is extremely low, even when compared to other Asian cities. However, there are still enough cars on the roads to make traffic jams a part of life in the Central District and Kowloon.

Most people use the well-developed public transportation system. A subway runs through a tunnel under Victoria Harbor, and construction continues on the rail system in other parts of Hong Kong. Other forms of public transportation include buses, ferries, and minibuses. Cable cars operate between Victoria Peak and the Central District.

Hong Kong's Kai Tak Airport is located on the eastern fringe of Kowloon and is one of the busiest airports in the world. In 1995, more than 27.4 million passengers passed through the airport. Since Kai Tak is already operating at full capacity, and air traffic is expected to increase, Hong Kong is in urgent need of a new airport. In 1991, British and Chinese authorities agreed to develop a new airport at Chek Lap Kok in the New Territories. The Airport Authority statutory body is responsible for the provision and construction of the new airport and will be responsible for the airport's future operation. When fully completed, the new airport at Chek Lap Kok will be able to serve 87 million passengers and handle 9.9 million tons (nine million tonnes) of cargo annually.

Above: **Technicians testing electronic products. Electronic goods are one of Hong Kong's major exports.**

Opposite: **The Lippo Center in the Central District houses many financial offices.**

INDUSTRY AND MANUFACTURING

As an international duty-free port, Hong Kong's trade flourished until 1951, when the United Nations placed an embargo on trade with communist China and North Korea. Chinese industrialists, many of them from Shanghai, avoided the UN embargo by emigrating to Hong Kong. They brought with them the technology, skilled labor, and capital that made possible Hong Kong's rapid industrial development.

Hong Kong–China trade later revived, bringing new opportunities for manufacturers. Foreign investment rapidly flowed in to take advantage of the territory's cheap and abundant labor and cheap raw materials from China. In March 1977, the Hong Kong Industrial Estates Corporation was established to develop and manage industrial estates that would accommodate high-tech industries.

Manufacturing employs almost 40% of the labor force and has become the most important sector of the Hong Kong economy. Textile and clothing production is the main manufacturing activity, employing almost 40% of industrial workers. Other major light manufacturing products are electronic goods, plastic goods (such as toys), watches and clocks, photographic equipment, and ornamental diamonds.

Some heavy industries, such as shipbuilding and aircraft engineering, are also developing. Hong Kong has developed an international reputation in these areas. Steel rolling, production of machine tools and parts, and cement manufacturing serve local needs.

FINANCIAL SERVICES

Hong Kong has developed into the leading financial center in Asia and third in the world after New York and London. There is no central bank; the major commercial banks and the government Banking Commissioner's Office work together to manage the territory's currency and interest rates. The territory's financial industry grew rapidly because the government imposes no restrictions on foreign exchange.

Hong Kong provides the financial infrastructure and wide range of services necessary to attract foreign banks. Eight-five of the world's 100 largest banks are represented in Hong Kong.

Domestic and international currencies are traded at the Hong Kong foreign exchange market. The foreign exchange market ranks fifth in the world and has a daily turnover of over US$90 billion.

The Stock Exchange of Hong Kong was established in 1986 to unite foreign stock exchange. The stock market represents a major source of capital for locally funded enterprises. It attracts investment from both foreign and domestic sources. The Hong Kong Futures Exchange trades in financial and commodity futures, such as gold and cotton.

HONG KONGERS

HONG KONG SOCIETY WAS MULTIRACIAL from the start, a reflection of the diverse nature of the British empire. For example, when Britain took possession of Hong Kong in 1841, there were almost 3,000 Indian soldiers among the British troops.

Since then, Hong Kong has absorbed people from all over the world. The ethnic Chinese form the majority of the population. There is, of course, a British community. In its early days, Hong Kong also attracted immigrants from the United States, Germany, Portugal, and Denmark, as well as Hindus, Muslims, Parsees, and Sikhs from India and Jews from Iraq. There are also Hong-Kong-born Eurasians—people of mixed European and Asian heritage.

The communities who populated Hong Kong boasted members from all walks of life. They were traders, lawyers, missionaries, shipbuilders, shopkeepers, soldiers, journalists, editors, bankers, and artists. Many of their descendants live in Hong Kong today. They are equally fluent in English and Cantonese—a turbaned Sikh man speaking fluent Cantonese would not merit a second glance in Hong Kong. The smaller communities have managed to keep their distinct identities and traditions while adapting to the majority culture.

Today, Hong Kong has a population of around 6.3 million. About 98% of the population are Chinese, and the remaining 2% are about evenly divided between Asians and non-Asians.

The territory has a population density of around 15,000 people per square mile (5,790 per square km). Some sections of Kowloon house 388,000 people per square mile (150,000 per square km), making them the most densely populated areas on earth.

Above: **Chinese and Indian Hong Kongers in a typing class.**

Opposite: **Hakka farming women wear distinctive hats to shade them from the sun.**

Chinese children with a lucky lion statue.

THE HONG KONG CHINESE

The overwhelming majority of Hong Kongers are Chinese. About one-third of Hong Kong Chinese were born in China. The Chinese population can be subdivided into groups based on which part of China they (or their ancestors) came from, and which dialect they speak.

CANTONESE Most of the early Chinese immigrants came from the southern Chinese province of Guangdong. They brought with them their dialect, Cantonese, and their customs. Hundreds of thousands of immigrants from Guangdong entered Hong Kong during the first half of the 20th century. Today, around 90% of Hong Kong Chinese are Cantonese.

Over the years, the Hong Kong Chinese have created their own identity that sets them apart from the Chinese of China or Taiwan. Because they have lived under British influence for so many years, they are perceived as being more Westernized. The Hong Kong Chinese were enjoying the material benefits of modernization—such as television and indoor plumbing—long before these were available in China or Taiwan. However, this modern veneer has not eliminated their cultural attitudes and traditions, which remain very Chinese.

When Hong Kong was a British colony, the Hong Kong Chinese asserted their distinct identity by retaining the Cantonese dialect, rather than adopting Putonghua, the national language of China and Taiwan, which is based on Mandarin, the dialect of Beijing. They also refused to adopt the simplified Chinese characters used in China and Taiwan. However, with the handover of the colony to China, the Hong Kong Chinese will have no choice but to conform to the standards of the mainland, which will mean learning Putonghua and possibly using the simplified characters.

OTHER DIALECT GROUPS A minority of Hong Kong Chinese—less than 10%—come from other dialect groups. These groups include the Hakka, Siyi, Chaochow, Hoklo, and Tanka. There are also significant numbers of Chinese from Shanghai and Fukien in China, and from Taiwan. There are smaller numbers of people from all over China. Almost all of them live a modern, urban lifestyle, but their heritage is revealed in the dialect they speak among themselves and the details of their cooking, ceremonies, religious practices, and other customs. The few people who retain a more traditional lifestyle, such as the Hakka farmers of the New Territories, may also have a distinctive style of dress.

A Chinese tailor in his shop.

OTHER ETHNIC GROUPS

Around 2% of the population of Hong Kong belong to ethnic groups other than Chinese. There are roughly equal numbers of Asians (including Indians, Filipinos, Japanese, Pakistanis, and Singaporeans) and non-Asians (including British, Americans, Australians, Canadians, and New Zealanders). Some are descended from early settlers in Hong Kong, while others live in Hong Kong as expatriates (usually defined as people who live outside their country by choice).

In Hong Kong, the term "expatriate" was once used to describe all non-Chinese, even those who were born in Hong Kong. On the other hand, ethnic Chinese, even if they were born outside Hong Kong, were not considered foreigners. This attitude changed slowly as Chinese Hong Kongers saw many non-Chinese residents becoming fluent in Cantonese and contributing to the territory's economy and administration.

An expatriate waitress dishes up Western food at Mad Dog's, an English-style tavern.

FOREIGN DEVILS

In Hong Kong, Westerners of Caucasian appearance are referred to as *gweilo* ("gwy-loh"), meaning "foreign devil" in Cantonese.

The ancient Chinese considered China to be the Middle Kingdom, midway between heaven and hell. Since non-Chinese could not be from heaven (which would mean that they were better than the Chinese), they must be from hell, hence the term "foreign devil." The Europeans' role in getting millions of Chinese addicted to opium probably reinforced this idea.

Although the term is understandably offensive, it is not intended as an insult. Today, the term gweilo is generally used simply because it has always been used. It is occasionally even used as a term of affection.

However, non-Chinese Hong Kongers were made to feel like foreigners in their own land when it was announced that only ethnic Chinese would be given Chinese citizenship in July 1997, when Hong Kong reverted to China. Some people whose families had been in Hong Kong for generations faced the prospect of becoming stateless. Those who have been fortunate enough to obtain British citizenship are able to remain in the Special Administrative Region. They can leave any time they want to, so they have adopted a wait-and-see attitude. Those who were not so fortunate have had to leave the only home they've known, emigrating to the United States, Canada, Singapore, and Malaysia, among other countries.

The Indian community is one of Hong Kong's oldest minority groups.

INDIANS Indians are a prominent group in Hong Kong's commercial and social scene. In the late 19th and early 20th centuries, Indian traders—mostly Dawoodi Bohras from Bombay and the state of Gujarat—came to Hong Kong in large numbers. They first worked with British traders and later set up business for themselves. They were joined by other Indian traders—Muslims, Hindus, and Parsees.

While the traditional occupation of most Hong Kong Indians is trade, the Sikhs usually came as part of a police or military force. Even today, Sikhs have the reputation of incorruptibility—Hong Kong's organized crime syndicates know that Sikhs cannot be enticed to rob their employers. For this reason, and because they are generally tall and strong, Sikhs are often employed as guards.

Although most are still traders, many third and fourth generation Hong Kong Indians have branched out into other occupations, ranging from academia and banking to the civil service.

Michael Kadoorie and his family. The Kadoories are prominent members of Hong Kong's Jewish community.

JEWS Among the earliest settlers in Hong Kong were Sephardic Jews from Iraq. Sephardic Jews follow the liturgy and customs of Jews of medieval Spain and Portugal. In the 15th century, they were expelled from Europe and settled in the Middle East and North Africa.

The Iraqi Jews were traders who came to Hong Kong and China by way of India. This merchant community enjoyed close personal and commercial ties with the Jewish communities in Shanghai and Bombay. Initially trading in cotton and other commodities, the Jews soon became involved in the opium trade. Eventually, they branched out into other areas, including real estate, banking, insurance, and hotels. This propelled them to power and influence both within Hong Kong and in the international business scene. Lord Lawrence Kadoorie, a member of Hong Kong's Jewish community, was the first person from the colony to have a seat in the United Kingdom's House of Lords.

EURASIANS Eurasian communities can be found in all the Asian countries colonized by Europeans. The word "Eurasian" reflects the mixed heritage of those descended from the union of European and Asian parents. Eurasians communities have distinct traditions, cuisine, and customs that differ slightly depending on the ethnic groups from which they were descended.

Interracial relationships were frowned on in the early years, and Eurasian children of mixed-race marriages faced considerable discrimination. The separate ethnic communities in Hong Kong were not comfortable with the idea of mixed marriages. However, since Eurasians were usually fluent in English, Cantonese, and possibly other languages of their parents, they were favored by the British colonial administration to fill posts in the civil service. Many Eurasian families in Hong Kong are among the island's wealthiest and most respected inhabitants.

In recent years, a new Eurasian community has grown, this time because a number of Hong Kongers have gone abroad for work or study and brought home European or American spouses.

Eurasian children on an amusement park ride.

LIFESTYLE

TO AN OUTSIDER, HONG KONG'S crowds, traffic jams, skyscrapers, and rows of concrete apartment buildings may seem overwhelming, but Hong Kongers have learned to deal with life in one of the most densely populated places on earth.

Hong Kong was carved out of a rocky island by people with ambition, determination, and the desire to succeed economically. This motivation can be seen today in Hong Kong's fiercely competitive business world. At the same time, traditional Chinese values and customs play an important role in everyday life.

FAMILY

The family is the strongest social unit in Hong Kong. Children are taught that respecting their family and their parents is their primary duty. This ensures that the family remains close-knit.

In the old days, the traditional family structure was an extended family living together under one roof. However, large families are no longer usual in Hong Kong, given the constraints of housing. It is now common for children to move to their own apartment when they marry and raise a family.

In the traditional family, the man was the head of the household. His word was law. He went out to earn a living while the woman tended to the home and children. Now that more and more women are educated, working, and financially independent, these family roles are changing. Women are resisting the traditional thinking that their place is in the home. The role of the head of the household is also changing. Children no longer

Above: **Boys take the plunge off a junk. Several thousand people live on boats around Hong Kong, but their numbers are dwindling.**

Opposite: **Crowds are an inevitable part of daily life in Hong Kong.**

accept the absolute authority of the father. Whereas the father used to make all the decisions, sons and daughters now expect a say in family matters.

The role of grandparents has also changed. In the traditional extended family, they were considered keepers of wisdom, and their opinions were sought and respected. As many of the elder generation now live apart from their children and grandchildren, their influence on the family has decreased.

These girls are enjoying a visit to a park with their grandmother. Although extended families are becoming less common, many grandparents still help to look after young children.

CONFUCIANISM

Confucian ethics are important to the people of Hong Kong.

Confucius (551–479 B.C.) was China's most famous and influential teacher and philosopher. Born at the time of the Warring States, he taught a system of morality and statecraft to bring about peace, stability, and just government. He is venerated as the man who established the code of conduct that is the basis for Chinese culture and lifestyle.

Confucianism is a system of ethical precepts for the management of society based on the practice of sympathy or "human-heartedness," demonstrated through a combination of etiquette and ritual. Confucius set out a code of behavior for five categories of relationships: loyalty of a subject to a ruler, a son to his father, a younger brother to an elder brother, a wife to her husband, and a friend to another friend. Respect and loyalty, an integral part of any relationship, are fundamental Confucian values that strengthen harmony.

Filial piety—meaning respect and obedience to one's family elders— is another important Confucian value. Filial piety is a cohesive force binding families together even in Westernized, modernized Hong Kong.

High-rise apartments are clustered along the coast at Wah Fu.

HOUSING

Housing has always been a problem in Hong Kong. It is estimated that over 40% of the territory's land area is unsuitable for development. As a result, most Hong Kong residents live in apartments. Property with its own land is uncommon, except among the very wealthy. Many of these properties are mansions scattered in and around the southern hills of Hong Kong Island. The middle class live at the base of the hills in 1,000 square foot (92 square meter) flats that cost an average of $1 million or more.

As Hong Kong developed and the population grew, housing costs were soon out of reach of the average resident. Hundreds of thousands of people lived in squalid shantytowns. In 1953, a shantytown fire left 53,000 people homeless. The government's emergency relocation measures soon became a full-scale public housing program. Construction on a massive scale resulted in the multi-story apartment blocks that can be seen everywhere today. The apartment blocks are a vast improvement over the old shantytowns, but they are still terribly overcrowded.

FUNG SHUI

Fung shui ("fung soy"), which means "wind and water," is a Chinese concept that is taken seriously by all residents of Hong Kong. Fung shui is about living in harmony with the natural environment and tapping the goodness of nature for good fortune and health. All Hong Kong residents understand the importance of good fung shui—for them, it is an essential ingredient for success.

Fung shui was first practiced in ancient China by farmers, for whom wind and water were important natural forces that had the power to either nurture or destroy their crops. The practice has developed into an art of positioning buildings and other structures—such as fountains, bridges, and graves—so that they harmonize with the surrounding environment. The invisible forces that the Chinese believe exist beneath the earth are measured by a specially designed compass. A balance of the negative (yin) and positive (yang) forces in the immediate surroundings is important for good health and fortune.

Fung shui practitioners examine all aspects of a structure. If the structure is an existing building, the fung shui master will suggest the best way to readjust the natural forces in order to reestablish balance, perhaps by rearranging the furniture, repainting the room a different color, or placing mirrors in front of doors in order to deflect negative energy. For a new building, the fung shui master's recommendations will range from the selection of the site and orientation of the building to the alignment of doors and windows and the placement of furniture.

The long-term strategy of the public housing program is to produce new housing and upgrade the older estates to meet the overwhelming demand. As land on Hong Kong Island and Kowloon becomes even scarcer and more expensive, new urban centers—"new towns"—have sprung up in outlying areas. Many people live on islands or in the New Territories and commute to work by ferry and train.

The Hong Kong Housing Authority (HKHA), which is responsible for the housing program, housed 53% of the population in 1996. The HKHA also finances the construction of schools, hospitals, and commercial buildings around the apartment blocks.

Hong Kong's public housing program offers a wide range of rental and home ownership schemes.

RICH AND POOR

In Hong Kong, there is a stark contrast in lifestyles between the rich and the poor. The super-rich of Hong Kong live in palatial homes and employ cooks, gardeners, chauffeurs, and other domestic servants. Many of the rich are Chinese people who have made money as factory owners, bankers, or merchants. The most popular neighborhood of the rich is Victoria Peak, high above the city with magnificent views of the harbor.

At the opposite end of the scale are the homeless people who can be spotted living under bridges and the squatters living in makeshift tents and cardboard homes at the edge of parks. Some of the older apartment blocks deteriorated into virtual slums; however, the government has demolished the worst blocks and is constantly working to improve housing standards. Hong Kong has virtually no social security system.

Models pose at a luxury car show. Hong Kong has more Rolls Royces per capita than any other place in the world.

WORKING LIFE

The life of most Hong Kong residents is dominated by work and the pursuit of money. The commercial beginnings of the colony, the emphasis on free trade, the shortage of land on which to farm, the influx of refugees determined to survive and prosper, and the lack of a social security system all contribute to an atmosphere where work and profit are among the highest priorities.

In search of economic security for themselves and their families, people work long hours and take on extra jobs. Being one's own boss is highly valued, so small businesses can be seen everywhere, from fruit stalls to fortune-tellers and roadside barbers. Where there is a need, someone will start a business to fill it. Some families work from home, taking on simple but monotonous manufacturing jobs, such as assembling toy parts. There are laws that prevent children under 14 from working in shops and factories, but in family businesses, even the children put in long hours to help the family survive.

A street sweeper at work on Lantau Island.

On the streets of Hong Kong, it seems that everyone is rushing to seal a business deal. Mobile phones are very popular, since they allow people to conduct business on the run. Peddlers, executives in suits, millionaires in limousines—everyone is out to make a dollar.

Farmers and fishers have a slower, quieter life, but they are still industrious. Women perform hard work in the fields, chatting to one another as they sift the soil and pull out weeds. Their lifestyle has barely changed in hundreds of years. However, many of the men in rural areas now work in industries in the towns, leaving the women to tend the farms.

A primary school class on Hong Kong Island.

EDUCATION

Education is a central tenet of Confucianism. Hong Kongers see education as the key to a better life for their children and for themselves, since parents rely on their children to look after them in their old age. As a result, education is taken very seriously by both parents and children. Children spend long hours studying at school and at home. Competition to get into the best high schools and universities is fierce.

Hong Kong has both government and private schools. Until 1971 even public elementary schools charged fees, but the government now provides nine years of free and compulsory education up to the age of 15. Chinese is the language of instruction in most schools. English is taught as a second language. There are also English-language schools and international schools that are open to children of all races.

After compulsory junior high school (grades 7–10), students take central examinations and are allocated places for grades 11 and 12, according to their rank. They may attend grammar, technical, or prevocational schools.

Students who wish to continue full-time education in Hong Kong have a choice of one teacher training college and seven universities, including the University of Hong Kong (English language) and the Chinese University of Hong Kong (Chinese language). Those whose families can afford it may choose to study overseas, often in Britain, the United States, or Canada. These days, many Hong Kong parents are choosing to send their children abroad in the hope that they can obtain permanent residence in these countries. This would offer their families a way out of Hong Kong if they decide they do not like living under Chinese administration.

Hong Kong has over 60 special schools for the visually, aurally, physically, emotionally, and mentally handicapped. The Ministry of Education tries as much as possible to integrate children with disabilities into the mainstream school system.

Schoolgirls wait for the bus home. After a day at school, Hong Kong teenagers must devote many hours to study if they hope to qualify for university.

FACE

"Face" is important concept in Chinese society. Keeping face means upholding a person's prestige in society. Losing face is to be avoided at all costs. A person could lose face by being ridiculed or reprimanded in public, which would result in a loss of prestige. Giving face—making sure not to inadvertently show someone up in public—is something children learn young

WEDDINGS

The actual marriage ceremony, which often takes place at the Registry of Marriages, is usually a simple affair, with only close family and friends in attendance. The traditional wedding banquet, however, is a different story.

Wedding banquets in Hong Kong are a measure of status. The larger and more elaborate the banquet, the more "face" the bride and groom and their families will have. The result is a sit-down dinner for hundreds of people in a huge hall or ballroom.

The other result of a huge wedding banquet is a huge bill. Traditionally, the banquet is the financial responsibility of the groom's family, as the banquet is a celebration to welcome the future mother of their grandchildren into the family. To help with the cost of the banquet, guests give *laisee* ("ly-see," red packets of lucky money) instead of gifts.

Wedding banquets are long, noisy affairs. The meal usually has 10-courses, which means that dinner lasts for two or three hours. Then there are the obligatory speeches. In the course of the evening, the bride will change from a Western-style white wedding gown to a red traditional outfit. The wedding couple go from table to table to toast their guests and receive lively toasts in return. Once dessert is served, it's time to go, and the bride and groom and their families stand at the door to see their guests off.

The most important part of the traditional wedding is the tea ceremony. This is when the new bride serves tea to all her in-laws older than her husband. Called *zham cha* ("tsum chah," literally "serve tea"), the tea ceremony is a way for the bride to show her respect to the elders in her new family. In ancient times, this was when the groom asked for approval of his choice of bride. If his parents did not approve, they would not accept tea from the couple. These days, family elders use it as an occasion to bestow their blessings on the couple.

FUNERALS

Like weddings, funerals in Hong Kong are an indicator of status. The more important and wealthy the deceased or the bereaved family, the more people there will be at the funeral. When the funeral service begins, the casket is wheeled into the funeral hall. Mourners are expected to walk around the casket to pay their last respects.

If the deceased was Christian, a Christian funeral service follows. If Buddhist or Taoist, the family holds a wake that may last for several days, with the priest burning incense and chanting prayers. After the funeral, in order to ensure that the deceased will have money and other luxury items in the afterlife, paper money and images of consumer goods, such as houses, cars, and washing machines, are burnt. It is believed that when these paper images burn, the smoke takes them up to heaven.

Above: **This elaborate paper house will be burned to ensure that the deceased has good housing in the afterlife.**

Opposite: **A happy bridal couple after the banquet. The bride is wearing traditional wedding clothes.**

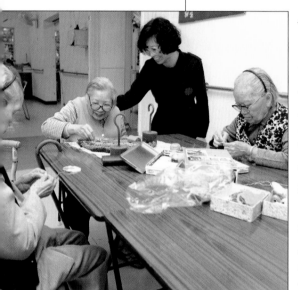

This rehabilitation center for elderly people is jointly run by the government and charitable organizations.

HEALTH CARE

Hong Kong residents enjoy good health due to the extensive preventive measures implemented by the government's community health services. These preventive services have contributed to Hong Kong's low infant and maternal mortality rates, which are among the best in the world. They have also kept Hong Kong, one of the most densely populated cities in the world, free from epidemics of major communicable diseases.

Hong Kong has government, government-assisted, and private hospitals. The Department of Health operates general outpatient clinics and maternal and child health centers throughout Hong Kong Island, Kowloon, and the New Territories. In addition, the Hospital Authority runs specialist outpatient clinics. Villagers in the remote areas of the New Territories are served by mobile dispensaries, and islanders are visited by "floating clinics." Helicopters provide a "flying doctor" service to the more isolated and inaccessible communities.

Cases of tuberculosis, leprosy, and venereal disease are given free treatment. Maternity and child health guidance, including prenatal and postnatal care and immunization, is also free. Family planning services are available at a charge of HK$1 for every visit. There are also free health care services that cater for the needs of children and adolescents at various stages of their development. Services include physical examination, health assessment, individual counseling, and health education.

Despite the successes of the health care system, the hospitals and clinics are under great pressure from overcrowding, and patients often have to wait many hours for treatment.

TRADITIONAL CHINESE MEDICINE

Although Western medicine is entirely acceptable to Chinese people in Hong Kong, many people still consult traditional Chinese medical practitioners.

Traditional Chinese medicine attempts to strengthen and balance the functioning of the entire body, rather than simply curing an ailment or alleviating symptoms. The physician diagnoses patients by taking their pulse, checking the color of their tongue, and evaluating their symptoms, which are linked to disorders of certain organs. Prescriptions, usually a combination of herbs, are given to the patients along with diet recommendations. The medicine usually has to be taken for a long period of time to be effective. The prescriptions occasionally include unusual ingredients, such as snakes, lizards, animal horns, and glands. The practice of using body parts from endangered animals, such as tigers from China and rhinoceroses from Africa, has brought some species close to extinction. International organizations are working to stamp out this illegal trade.

Acupuncture is perhaps the best-known Chinese medical practice in the West. Acupuncture is based on the theory that the body has an interlocking grid of energy lines. A person who feels unwell has either an imbalance of *yang* or *yin* (positive or negative energies) or an uneven distribution of *chi* (life energy). In order to bring the chi back into balance, the body is pierced at specific points, at various angles and to various depths, with special needles. There have been many documented cases of successful treatment using acupuncture.

RELIGION

MOST HONG KONG CHINESE practice a mix of Buddhism, Taoism, and Confucianism. Some people even combine these beliefs with Christianity, going to church on Sunday and then visiting a temple to burn joss sticks (incense sticks) for good luck. Animism can still be found; offerings or joss sticks are placed at the foot of certain rocks and trees that are believed to house spirits. Hong Kongers are very tolerant of different religious beliefs.

Buddhism and Taoism were introduced to Hong Kong by immigrants from the mainland. Some Buddhist and Taoist temples date back over seven centuries, while others were built in recent years with all the magnificence of traditional Chinese architecture. In all, there are more than 600 Buddhist and Taoist temples in the territory. There are also almost 800 Christian churches and chapels, four mosques, a Hindu temple, a Sikh temple, and a Jewish synagogue.

In the New Territories, many villages retain traditional clan organizations. They have an ancestral hall where tablets inscribed with ancestors' names are kept and venerated. The hall is the center of both religious and secular activities among villagers.

Left: **Teenage girls worshiping at Wong Tai Sin Temple, a Taoist temple in Kowloon.**

Opposite: **A statue of Kwan Yin, the Buddhist Goddess of Mercy, stands at Repulse Bay. Other leading deities include Kwan Tai, God of War and the source of righteousness; Pak Tai, Supreme Emperor of the Dark Heaven and patron of the island of Cheung Chau; and Hung Shing, God of the South Seas and a weather prophet.**

Prayers, candles, incense, and fruit are offered at Buddhist and Taoist temples.

BUDDHISM AND TAOISM

Buddhism was founded in India in the 6th century B.C. by Prince Siddhartha Gautama. Gautama, disillusioned by the misery and injustice he saw in the world, renounced his royal heritage to seek enlightenment, which he attained after meditating for many years. "Buddha" means "Enlightened One." Buddha taught that the source of human suffering and misery is craving and desires, and that meditation to eliminate desires can lead to spiritual enlightenment. Buddhism became established as a major religion in China in the 6th century A.D.

Taoism originated in China around 2,500 years ago. Its founder was Lao Tzu ("Teacher" or "Old One"). Taoism advocates a life of simplicity and passivity following the *tao* ("tow," rhymes with "how")—the guiding path that leads to immortality. Many people who lived in harmony with nature, including Lao Tzu, are now worshiped as Taoist gods.

Both Buddhism and Taoism was brought to Hong Kong by immigrants from the mainland, and their practices have merged to some extent. Among the Buddhist and Taoist believers, almost every household has its ancestral shrine, and countless shops have a "God Shelf" with images of the owner's favorite deities. Traditional rites associated with birth, marriage, death, and festivals are still widely observed. Temples are especially crowded during festivals and on the first and 15th days of lunar months. Although each temple is generally dedicated to one or occasionally two deities, it is common for images of multiple deities to be displayed. Taoist priests perform elaborate rites, offering thanks to the gods and praying for prosperity and happiness.

Religious studies are conducted in monasteries, nunneries, and hermitages. Hong Kong's best known monasteries are situated in the more remote parts of the New Territories. The Buddhist Po Lin Monastery on Lantau Island is renowned for its view of the sunrise and for its gigantic Buddha statue.

Taoist and Buddhist organizations help to meet welfare, educational, and medical needs in Hong Kong, either directly or by contributing to charitable organizations.

The popular Man Mo Temple is run by a local charitable organization and is dedicated to the Gods of Literary Attainment and Martial Valor. The huge incense coils that hang from the ceiling are donated by pious worshipers.

TIN HAU, A GODDESS OF THE SEA

Since Hong Kong has always depended on the sea, originally for fishing and then for trade, the most popular deities are those connected with the sea and the weather. It is estimated that Tin Hau, the "Queen of Heaven" and protector of seafarers, is worshiped by 250,000 people. There are at least 24 Tin Hau temples in Hong Kong, the earliest and most famous being the one at Fat Tong Mun in Joss House Bay.

St. John's Cathedral in the Central District.

CHRISTIANITY

Christianity in Hong Kong dates back almost to the founding of the territory. The first church was established in 1841. Today, there are 52 Christian denominations and independent groups in Hong Kong. The Christian community is estimated at more than 500,000.

A Roman Catholic church was established in Hong Kong in 1841. Hong Kong became a diocese in 1946. In 1969, Francis Chen-peng Hsu became Hong Kong's first Chinese bishop. The present bishop, John Baptist Cheng-chung Wu, was consecrated in 1975 and became a cardinal in 1988. There are 62 parishes and 35 centers for Mass. Services are conducted in Chinese, with a few churches providing services in English.

One of the prime concerns of the diocese has been for the well-being of all the people of Hong Kong. There are 327 Catholic schools and kindergartens administered by the Catholic Board of Education. Catholic medical and social services include hospitals, clinics, social centers, hostels, homes for the aged, a home for the handicapped, and many self-help clubs and associations. These services are open to people of all faiths.

The Protestant community also dates back to 1841. The Baptists form the largest denomination, followed by the Lutherans. Other major denominations are the Adventist, Anglican, Christian and Missionary Alliance, Church of Christ in China, Methodist, and Pentecostal churches. Due to their emphasis on youth work, many congregations have a high proportion of young people. Since the 1970s, the number of independent churches has increased significantly due to the evangelical zeal of lay Christians.

The Protestant churches are involved in education, health care, and social welfare. Protestant organizations operate three tertiary colleges, 131 secondary schools, 141 primary schools, and 143 kindergartens. In addition, they operate theological seminaries and Bible institutes, Christian publishing houses, and Christian bookshops. They run hospitals, clinics, and social service organizations that provide a wide range of social services including community and youth centers, day care centers, children's homes, homes for the elderly, schools for the deaf, training centers for the mentally handicapped, and camp sites.

A Sunday-morning song and prayer meeting.

A Chinese Muslim reads the Koran.

OTHER RELIGIONS

ISLAM There are approximately 50,000 Muslims in Hong Kong. The majority are Chinese, with the rest mainly from Pakistan, India, Malaysia, Indonesia, the Middle East, and Africa. There are three mosques on Hong Kong Island and one in Kowloon. The Shelley Street Masjid was the first to be built in Hong Kong, in the 1840s. The Kowloon Masjid and Islamic Center can accommodate about 2,000 worshipers.

The Incorporated Trustees of the Islamic Community Fund of Hong Kong—an organization made up of the Islamic Union of Hong Kong, the Pakistan Association, the Indian Muslim Association, and the Dawoodi Bohra Association—coordinates religious affairs and manages mosques and Muslim cemeteries.

Charitable work among the Muslim community, including financial aid to the needy, medical care, educational assistance, the provision of an Islamic kindergarten, and assistance for the aged, is conducted through various Muslim organizations in Hong Kong.

HINDUISM The religious and social activities of Hong Kong's 12,000-strong Hindu community are centered in the Hindu Temple in Happy Valley on Hong Kong Island. The Hindu Association of Hong Kong is responsible for the upkeep of the temple, which is used for the observance of Hindu festivals and for meditation, spiritual lectures, yoga classes, devotional music sessions, and other community activities. Naming, engagement, and marriage ceremonies are performed at the temple according to Hindu rites. Other important services rendered by the temple include administration of last rites, cremation ceremonies, and the upkeep of the Hindu crematorium at Cape Collinson.

Khalsa Diwan Sikh temple.

SIKHISM Hong Kong has a small Sikh community. A unique feature of the Sikh Temple is that it provides free meals and short-term accommodation to overseas visitors of any faith.

JUDAISM Hong Kong's Jewish community worships at the Synagogue Ohel Leah, the American Club, and several other locations. The synagogue was built in 1901 on land given by Sir Jacob Sassoon and his family. The original site included a rabbi's residence and school, as well as a recreation club for the 1,000 people in the congregation. There is also a Jewish Cemetery. The site adjoining the synagogue, which once housed the school and club, has been redeveloped into two residential blocks of flats. Within this complex is the new Jewish Community Center which has recreational and kosher dining facilities. The center has a specialist library carefully put together to cover all aspects of Judaism.

LANGUAGE

THE OFFICIAL LANGUAGES OF HONG KONG are English and Chinese. Both languages possess equal status in communications between the government and the public. This is provided for in the Official Languages Ordinance, enacted in 1974. Major reports and government publications of public interest are available in both English and Chinese. Simultaneous interpretation is provided at meetings of all government boards and committees. Government departments reply to correspondence from the public in either English or Chinese—whichever language the correspondence comes in. All new principal legislation enacted since 1989 is in both languages.

Above: **The Chinese take their handwriting seriously, as it reflects on their upbringing and character. Children spend hours practicing writing in order to develop and perfect a style that is easily decipherable yet graceful and esthetically appealing.**

Opposite: **Neon signs line Temple Street on the Kowloon peninsula.**

China is a huge country, and over the centuries many distinct dialects of Chinese have developed. A speaker of one dialect may not understand a speaker from a different part of China. Written Chinese, however, is the same for all dialects. The common spoken dialect in Hong Kong is Cantonese, the dialect of the Guangdong province of China.

Prior to 1974, English was the only official language, and English has always been the key to employment in the civil service and major corporations. This situation began to change, however, as Hong Kong prepared for the reversion to China. The government is encouraging more proficient use of Chinese in the civil service. The ultimate objective is to develop a civil service that is proficient in Cantonese, Putonghua (the official language of China, commonly called Mandarin), and English.

Non-Cantonese Hong Kongers usually speak their own language or dialect among themselves. However, almost all the people born and raised in Hong Kong can speak Cantonese, regardless of their race.

Friends gather in the park to converse and read newspapers.

SPOKEN CHINESE

With well over a billion speakers worldwide, Chinese is the most widely spoken language in the world. However, it is said to be a difficult language for non-Chinese to learn. The sounds of the words are difficult to master, and the writing system is very complex.

Chinese has eight major dialects—Mandarin, Cantonese, Wu, Hakka (or Kejia), Xiang, Gan, northern Min, and southern Min. The most important dialects in Hong Kong are Cantonese and Mandarin.

Cantonese is the common dialect of Hong Kong. Although Cantonese originated in the Guangdong province of China, the people of Hong Kong have their own distinctive style of speech. Cantonese is the language of the streets, and it is also the language of Hong Kong's popular culture, including movies and songs.

In China, Mandarin is spoken by at least 70% of the Han people, who constitute more than 90% of the total population. The official language of China is based on the Mandarin of Beijing and is known as Putonghua, or "common speech." References to standard Chinese, or simply to Chinese, are usually to Putonghua.

Chinese is a tonal language, meaning that the same syllable can have different meanings depending on the way it is pronounced. For example, by speaking in different tones (such as rising, falling, high, or low), the syllable *ma* in Putonghua can mean mother, hemp, horse, or scold. Putonghua has four distinct tones, while Cantonese has nine.

Both Chinese and Cantonese have an abundance of homonyms (words that sound the same but have different meanings—for example, *meet* and *meat*). In Hong Kong, when a word sounds like something auspicious, it takes on a special significance. The word for "bat" is *fu*, which sounds like the word *fu*, meaning "good luck." "Fish" (*yu*) sounds like "plenty" (*yu*). As a result, bats and fish are considered lucky creatures, and they feature in all sorts of designs and decorations. On the other hand, the number "four" is considered unlucky because it sounds like "death" in Cantonese.

Learn to count in Cantonese:
one – yat
two – yih
three – sam
four – sei
five – ngh
six – luk
seven – chat
eight – baat
nine – gau
ten – sahp

COMMON CANTONESE EXPRESSIONS

Zhang ("tsang") – cool, neat, fine, or excellent. It can apply to situations, people, or objects. You can have *zhang* cars, *zhang* clothes, and *zhang* books. When applied to people, it means that they are physically attractive. *Ho zhang wo* adds emphasis—really cool or excellent.

Yau mo gau cho ("yow mo gow cho") – literally, "What was messed up?" It's a good phrase to use when frustrated about things that other people mess up, or when things aren't going your way.

Lei po ("lay poh") – ridiculous. If you're really frustrated with the situation, you can say *lei sai po* ("lay sy poh").

Whereas English letters spell out the sounds of a word, a single Chinese character represents a complete idea (in this case, the idea of "full").

WRITTEN CHINESE

Although spoken Chinese dialects may differ enormously, all literate Chinese speakers can communicate with each other in writing, as all Chinese characters are written the same way, regardless of dialect. This makes it easier for the Chinese government to disseminate information about policies in Hong Kong—they are able to reach Cantonese-speaking Hong Kongers in writing.

Written Chinese is based on ideograms, meaning that each character is a pictorial representation of an idea. For example, the Chinese character for mountain is a simplified line drawing of a mountain. In the early stages of the language, one ideogram represented one word. As more words entered the language, two or more elements were combined to form a new ideogram. Sometimes two ideograms represent one idea. There are over 50,000 characters in written Chinese. Of these, about 3,000 are in common use. The simplest character has only one stroke, while the most complicated has 30. Not surprisingly, it is common for Chinese speakers to reach for a dictionary to look up characters they have not seen before, or that they have forgotten how to write.

Believing that the writing system was too complicated for the average person, the Chinese government introduced a simplified form of Chinese characters in 1964. The simplified characters keep the basic shape and meaning of the original characters but have fewer strokes. In Hong Kong, however, the traditional form has been retained.

DEALING WITH ENGLISH AND PUTONGHUA

Even though most high school students in Hong Kong study English as a first or second language, the general standard of spoken English in the colony is poor. This is mainly because very few children speak or hear English outside the classroom. English is a foreign language for most Hong Kong Chinese. However, mastery of English is still viewed as an essential step towards getting a good job or emigrating. This translates into a reasonably high demand for English-medium schools. There are also language schools that teach English conversation and business English to adults who wish to improve their job prospects.

Many emigrants from Hong Kong who have settled in English-speaking environments around the world quickly come to realize that the English they learned in school is really a mix of English and Cantonese that isn't very useful outside of Hong Kong. Many end up hiring a private tutor to help them communicate in their new place of residence.

Today Hong Kong residents have to learn Putonghua, the official language of China, in addition to English. Although the writing system is the same for Cantonese and Putonghua, the spoken language is completely different. Learning to speak it is supposedly as difficult as learning English. Putonghua is currently taught from the third year of primary school until the third year of secondary school. Starting in 1998, it will be taught from the first year of school until the last.

TELEVISION

Hong Kong has four local television channels that command a total daily audience of 5.8 million. This means that nearly every resident of Hong Kong watches television daily. The main broadcasters are Television Broadcasts Ltd (TVB) and Asia Television Ltd (ATV). Both provide separate Chinese and English language services.

Satellite television first came to Hong Kong in 1991, when Star TV was broadcast to the entire Asian region. Star TV provides sports, music, news, and Hindi and Chinese programs.

Cable television was introduced to Hong Kong only in 1993, when Wharf Cable launched its service with an initial eight channels. By 1995, this had expanded to 20 channels, including four pay-per-view movie channels. Wharf was the first station in the world to launch its own 24-hour Chinese news service and topped that by introducing a News-on-Demand service (via telephone) in 1994.

NEWSPAPERS AND MAGAZINES

At last count, there were about 800 publications registered in Hong Kong. At least 82 of these are newspapers, including 38 Chinese-language dailies, 10 English dailies, and several bilingual and other language papers.

The Chinese-language dailies mainly cover general news, both local and overseas. Some specialize in entertainment, especially television and movie news and horse racing. The larger papers are distributed to Chinese communities overseas.

Periodicals also do a booming business in Hong Kong. There are 674 publications registered, of which 374 are in Chinese, 158 in English, 125 bilingual, and 17 in other languages. These range from current affairs periodicals to technical journals and entertainment guides.

Hong Kong is the Southeast Asian base of operations for many international and regional magazines, news agencies, and newspapers. International news agencies such as the Associated Press are represented. International papers, such as the *Asian Wall Street Journal* and the *International Herald Tribune,* and international current affairs magazines, such as *Newsweek*, have locally printed editions. Hong Kong is also the base for the regional magazines *Asiaweek* and the *Far Eastern Economic Review.*

Above: **Literally hundreds of magazines are available in Hong Kong.**

Opposite: **A television crew from ATV.**

FREEDOM OF THE PRESS

Despite the Basic Law's guarantee of "freedom of speech, of the press, and of publication," some observers are anticipating major changes in Hong Kong's media scene. The People's Republic of China has a poor record when it comes to free speech. The media are not permitted to criticize the Communist Party or the government, and journalists may be convicted of espionage and jailed for long periods, even for life, if they fall out of favor with the government. The official Chinese news agency, Xinhua, has the right to censor news. Hong Kong's huge media industry, which is said to be the freest in Asia, is waiting to see how these policies will be applied in the SAR.

ARTS

HONG KONG HAS A LIVELY arts scene. Every year, Hong Kong residents can enjoy hundreds of cultural events, from traditional Chinese opera, puppet shows, and classical music performances to Western ballet and theater. The Hong Kong Philharmonic Orchestra, the Hong Kong Chinese Orchestra, the Chung Ying Theater Company, and the City Contemporary Dance Company are among the best known local artistic groups. Art exhibitions show the work of local and international painters and sculptors. Hong Kong is a major center for the sale of Asian art and antiques. Hollywood Road in the Central District is crowded with antique and curio shops, and major auction houses such as Sotheby's and Christie's have offices in Hong Kong. Hong Kong is also the hub of thriving Cantonese movie and music industries that export cultural products to the rest of Asia and, increasingly, the world.

Left: **The Hong Kong Cultural Center, located on the tip of the Kowloon peninsula.**

Opposite: **Ornate and colorful Chinese temple decorations.**

CALLIGRAPHY

The Chinese have developed calligraphy into an art form. In earlier centuries, scholars had to master calligraphy in order to pass the all-important civil service examinations, and the Chinese still place great importance on good handwriting.

All that is required for Chinese calligraphy is a brush, ink stick, ink stone, and paper. Calligraphers write poems, couplets, or proverbs. A well-written calligraphic piece plays on the senses, with the strokes invoking images of strength, beauty, or grace. Even if one does not know what the characters mean, the piece still has esthetic value.

Chinese calligraphy requires both physical and mental control.

There are several forms of calligraphy. The formal style has angular characters and few curved lines. Characters written in the "grass" style are more flowing and cursive. Only those who have studied Chinese calligraphy intensively can decipher the characters written in this style.

PAINTING

Chinese paintings are usually done on silk or absorbent paper. There are five categories of subjects: human figures, landscapes, flowers, birds and animals, and fish and insects. A pointed brush is used to apply the paint. Some styles use only black paint, while others are more colorful.

Chinese artists do not have a model in front of them when they paint. They paint from memory and finish their work quickly and confidently in a few minutes. Once completed, the artist may paint the picture again and again until he or she achieves the desired effect. Chinese artists attempt to capture the spirit of what they paint, not simply the image. To that end, artists sometimes spend hours meditating before putting their brush to paper. Many artists are known for only painting one subject, such as horses or birds.

Artists are evaluated on their brush strokes. Brush strokes are given special names, and critics examine how the brush strokes contribute to the effect of the picture. Calligraphy in the form of a couplet or a short stanza of poetry is almost always used to complete a painting, as it is believed to complement the picture.

Painting flowers on a folding paper fan.

Painted porcelain for sale in an antique shop on Hollywood Road.

FINE ARTS

The Chinese are well known for their decoration of porcelain and ceramic. Vases, urns, bowls, and plates are decorated with symbols of nature, seasons, or myths. Sometimes they are decorated with calligraphy. Perhaps the best known is the Ming style of blue and white porcelain.

Cloisonné is another popular fine art. Cloisonné is the method of decorating metal surfaces with enamel. Metal pieces are attached to a base plate, forming sections that are filled in with enamel paint. When the piece is heated, the enamel fuses to the metal, forming a glossy colored surface. Although the art was introduced to China from the Middle East, the Chinese perfected the technique. These days, cloisonné decorates everything from chairs to chopsticks.

The Chinese are also masters of carving. Jade, ivory, and rosewood are intricately carved. Sometimes knives as small as toothpicks are used for the finer work. Carved rosewood furniture inlaid with intricate mother-of-pearl designs are popular items.

CHINESE OPERA

Chinese opera started out as street performances where gongs, cymbals, and drums were used to attract the audience. Even today, these instruments herald the beginning of a new scene. The plots of the operas are taken from historical tracts, folk legends, classical novels, and fairy tales. There is a combination of singing, dramatic speech, acrobatics, and dancing. Accompanying the action and singing is a orchestra made up of Chinese fiddles, flutes, clappers, drums, cymbals, and gongs.

Chinese opera stages are usually quite bare, with only minimal props. Chairs may represent hills. A flag with the character for river on it represents a body of water. However, the dazzling and intricately embroidered costumes and glittery headgear more than make up for the lack of scenery. Male and female characters wear robes with long, wide sleeves. The sleeves are used for flirting and for showing fear or anger. The actors' makeup is very heavy and elaborate, with different colors signifying different character traits, such as loyalty or cleverness. Gods and fairies have gold or silver makeup. Yellow is the color of emperors, and green represents a person of high rank.

Operas usually last for several hours. Families turn up by the busload, bringing enough food and drink to last through the performance. The atmosphere is festive, and the action is not limited to the actors on stage. Spectators who stand up and join in the chorus or comment loudly on the action are at least as entertaining as the actors!

Chinese opera performers use dramatic gestures and sing in a high-pitched falsetto. Perfecting this vocal style requires years of dedicated practice.

CHINESE ORCHESTRAS

Traditional Chinese music is popular with the older population of Hong Kong. Hong Kong's 85-member Chinese Orchestra holds regular concerts at the Cultural Center and in other halls throughout the territory.

Traditional musical instruments include the *erhu* ("ER-hoo," a two-stringed fiddle), *yue chin* ("YOO-eh chin," a four-stringed banjo), *kucheng* ("KOO-chuhng," a zither), *hu chin* ("HOO chin," a two-stringed violin), and *pipa* ("PEE-pah," a four-stringed lute).

Traditional Chinese music is difficult for the uninitaiated to appreciate. In order to appeal to a wider range of tastes, including Western audiences, the traditional instruments are being modified, accompanied by western instruments such as the cello, and used experimentally to perform modern compositions.

An ensemble of traditional Chinese instruments.

CANTOPOP

Hong Kong is the center of a thriving Cantonese pop music industry, commonly called "Cantopop." Cantopop is based on Western popular musical forms, rather than traditional Chinese music.

Cantopop stars have a huge following among Chinese teenagers in Hong Kong, Taiwan, Singapore, and other Chinese-speaking communities, and they also have many fans in Asian countries such as Japan, even among people who don't speak Cantonese. Many of the singers record songs in Putonghua; some even record in Japanese.

Among the biggest stars of Cantopop are the four solo male singers whose popularity has earned them the title of "Heavenly Kings"—Andy Lau, Aaron Kwok, Jacky Cheung, and Leon Lai. Major female stars include Faye Wong, Sandy Lam, and Cass Phang. Although these singers are virtually unknown outside Asia, the top performers (such as Jacky Cheung) are among the biggest-selling artists in the world, selling as many records as Michael Jackson or Madonna.

Andy Lau is one of the "Heavenly Kings" of Hong Kong popular music. The hairstyles, dress, and mannerisms of the big Cantopop stars are widely imitated.

MOVIES

Hong Kong is the world's largest producer of Chinese-language action movies. Hong Kong also exports its movies all over Asia, even to non-Chinese speaking countries. Recently, Hong Kong movies have gained a following in the United States. Many Hong Kong stars are now household names around the world. Here are some of them:

JACKIE CHAN is the reigning king of Hong Kong action cinema, thanks to his comedy martial arts movies. He now has a huge following in the United States and recently received an MTV lifetime achievement award.

CHOW YUEN FAT was Hong Kong's most popular actor and probably its most prolific. Chow acted in movies of every genre, and worked closely with director John Woo.

BRUCE LEE, born Lee Sui Lung, was a movie legend. He was probably the first Chinese martial arts actor to become a well-known figure in the West and a household name around Asia. His son Brandon followed in his footsteps in more ways than one—they both died mysteriously at a young age.

JOHN WOO earned himself a place in film history with his masterful direction of Hong Kong action pictures. He has recently achieved huge success in Hollywood with films such as *Broken Arrow*. Woo's style is distinctive. His best known films, *The Killer*, *Bullet in the Head*, and *Hard Boiled*, show characters struggling with questions of loyalty and honor. They are punctuated by elaborately choreographed action sequences. Film festivals, independent movie theaters, video-tapes, and laser discs have brought his work to a legion of new fans.

Women in Hong Kong cinema are not relegated to soft roles. They are often central characters in kung fu movies, wielding swords, doing acrobatics, and felling bad guys with the best of them. Some of the better known are Maggie Cheung, Anita Mui, and Anita Yuen.

Above: **Bruce Lee in action.**

Opposite: **John Woo on the set of** *Broken Arrow.*

THE SHAW BROTHERS

There are several Shaw brothers, but the best known are Runme Shaw and Sir Runrun Shaw. They began Hong Kong's oldest film studio and thereby set in motion an industry that has made Hong Kong Asia's Hollywood.

Sir Runrun was a pioneer in Hong Kong filmmaking, producing Hong Kong's first movie with sound. The Shaw Brothers studios became the hub of activity in the film industry during the 1960s and 1970s. Many great action stars and directors began at the studio, which at the time was one of the largest and most advanced in Asia. The Shaw movie empire was exported to other countries in Asia and successfully branched out into distribution and exhibition of movies.

LEISURE

THE PEOPLE OF HONG KONG do not have a lot of time to spend on leisure, because they are busy working during the week. Most leisure activities are confined to weekends. Workdays are long: offices open at 8:30 a.m. and most people leave work between 6 and 7 p.m. Then there is the long commute home, which may take an hour or more. Schoolchildren do not have much more leisure time than their parents, because after-school hours are filled with homework and studying. At most, people may spend an hour or so watching television.

Above: **Expatriates enjoy a day out on a pleasure boat.**

Opposite: **On sunny mornings, Chinese men bring caged birds to the park and gather to hear them sing.**

On weekends, though, Hong Kongers engage in leisure activities with the same energy they put into working. Families picnic in the park, visit the outlying islands, go to the amusement park, or go swimming and sunning at the beach. Weekends are also the time for the family to eat out, perhaps to indulge in special dishes that are too time-consuming to prepare at home. Cinemas show local and foreign movies for all tastes.

Those who prefer more strenuous forms of leisure play any number of sports, including golf, cricket, soccer, tennis, and squash. Courts and sports grounds are provided by the Urban Council and other government organizations. The wealthy enjoy pleasure boating, sailing, and water-skiing in Hong Kong's many inlets and bays.

The elderly, who generally have more leisure time on their hands, may spend it playing board games. The two most popular board games are Chinese chess and *weiqi* ("way-chee"). Mahjong, a game played with tiles, is also phenomenally popular. This is partly because it involves gambling, one of Hong Kong's most popular leisure activities. For many people, gambling is a passion.

GOVERNMENT LEISURE PROGRAMS

In recent years, the people of Hong Kong have been able to pursue an increasing variety of recreational activities in their leisure time. Government programs to provide sports and other recreational facilities continue to expand each year, and thousands of events attract enthusiastic participants and supporters.

Sporting activities are coordinated by such organizations as the Urban Council, the Regional Council, the Home Affairs Department, the Hong

The 60-mile (100-km) "Trailwalker" charity walk is a popular annual event.

Kong Sports Institute, the Hong Kong Sports Development Board, and many voluntary associations. These organizations operate indoor games halls, soccer pitches, roller-skating rinks, jogging tracks, tennis courts, basketball courts, volleyball courts, squash courts, badminton courts, hockey fields, rugby grounds, outdoor and indoor stadiums, children's playgrounds, camping grounds, beaches, swimming pool complexes, parks and gardens, aviaries, and a zoo. They also provide indoor recreational facilities such as art and craft rooms.

PARK OUTINGS

Hong Kong has many parks throughout Hong Kong Island, Kowloon, and the New Territories. The country park system covers 40% of the land area.

A man relaxing with his chihuahuas.

Parks are important venues for leisure activities. Almost every day, urban parks are full of people walking, exercising, or just relaxing. On weekends, families go to the park to enjoy the fresh air and time spent with one another. On weekdays, early mornings are the busiest time. This is when young and old come to exercise before going to work or school. Groups of people practice martial arts. Children play games such as badminton. Older men sit under the trees playing Chinese chess.

On Sundays, parks are often the sites of fairs. The streets are cordoned off, and people crowd around the ice-cream and soda stalls and enjoy free performances. More remote parks are used for kite-flying, picnicking, hiking, cycling, and camping.

An instructor leads a tai chi class. Tai chi can be practiced with or without implements such as swords and fans.

TAI CHI

Every morning Hong Kong is full of people practicing tai chi ("ty chee"). Tai chi is a Chinese martial art primarily practiced for health. Tai chi emphasizes complete relaxation and is essentially a form of meditation. It has been called "meditation in motion." Unlike the hard martial arts, tai chi is characterized by soft, slow, flowing movements—which are nevertheless precisely executed—that emphasize force, rather than brute strength.

Tai chi traces its roots back to yoga, which was introduced to China from India. It gradually evolved into a Chinese martial art. In the 13th century, a Taoist monk adapted the martial art into what has come to be known as tai chi. Over the centuries, different style of tai chi evolved. The Yang style is the most common traditional style of tai chi practiced today.

The "chi" in tai chi refers to an ancient Chinese concept of energy. According to the philosophy of tai chi, this energy, or chi, flows throughout the body, but it can become blocked, causing the body to fall ill. There are several means of freeing up the flow of chi. Two of the more commonly known forms in the West are acupuncture and tai chi.

In addition to its physical benefits, tai chi is believed to have certain psychological effects as well. As a form of meditation, it is intended to help people understand themselves and to enable them to deal with others more effectively. Tai chi is based on the Taoist belief that there are two opposing principles in the universe—yin and yang. By restoring the balance of yin and yang through tai chi, people can improve their physical and spiritual well-being.

While tai chi used to be practiced mainly by the elderly, it has now caught on with the younger generation as well, as a means of relieving their urban stress.

The slow, meditative movements of tai chi give a sense of harmony to this scene.

LEE LAI SHAN, OLYMPIC CHAMPION

Although Hong Kong has been sending athletes to the Olympics Games since 1952, the territory won a medal for the first time in 1996, when Lee Lai Shan won a gold medal for windsurfing at the Atlanta Games. Lee is now a hero in Hong Kong. Hundreds of people crowded the airport to welcome her home, and thousands more lined the route of her motorcade as she made her way to the harbor for the last stretch of her journey to the island of Cheung Chau, where she lives. When she arrived on the island, she found that the inhabitants of the island had covered the planks of the wooden jetty with a huge red carpet. She was welcomed with numerous streamers and banners, as well as a lion dance and a band.

Ocean Park's Water World is Asia's largest water park.

BEACHES, POOLS, AND OCEAN PARK

Swimming is Hong Kong's most popular form of summer recreation. Forty-three beaches have been designated by the government as safe for aquatic activities. Beaches where sharks have been spotted are off limits. There are also 27 public swimming pool complexes throughout Hong Kong Island, Kowloon, and the New Territories. Four of these are heated pools for use in winter.

One of the most popular vacation activities for kids and adults is a visit to Ocean Park. Located on Hong Kong Island, Ocean Park combines both oceanarium and amusement park facilities. It has a range of rides, such as ferris wheels and roller coasters. Ocean Park also boasts the educational Dinosaur Discovery Trail, the Goldfish Pagoda, and the Butterfly House. It has a 738-foot (225-m) outdoor escalator, two aviaries, a bird theater, and a cultural village that teaches children about Chinese history, arts, crafts, mythology, customs, and inventions.

NIGHTLIFE

Hong Kong has long been known for its nightlife. Areas such as Tsim Sha Tsui, on the tip of the Kowloon peninsula, and Wanchai, on Hong Kong Island, are crowded with bars, nightclubs, pubs, and restaurants. There are also dozens of hostess bars and Chinese ballrooms, where customers buy a ticket to dance with a woman. Some of these establishments are very expensive and cater mainly to big-spending tourists, sailors on shore leave, and foreign businessmen on company expense accounts. However, there are still plenty of places where Hong Kongers go to enjoy themselves. Clubs offer a range of live music, including jazz, blues, and rock, and there are many discos. Imports such as Planet Hollywood, Hard Rock Café, and British-style pubs are becoming increasingly popular among young people.

One of the most popular varieties of nightlife is the karaoke bar. Karaoke ("ka-ra-OH-kay") is a Japanese word meaning "empty orchestra." People sing along to music videos that feature instrumental versions of popular songs. The lyrics are shown on the screen, and the karaoke aficionado follows along. Karaoke has proved so popular that many bars and nightclubs now offer karaoke services.

Karaoke clubs offer private rooms with television sets, karaoke videos, and a microphone. Groups of friends can rent one of these private karaoke rooms for a sing-along.

A group of friends at a local tea shop, absorbed in their game of mahjong.

MAHJONG

Mahjong, an ancient Chinese game with many variations, is a popular pastime in Hong Kong. A mahjong set of tiles is the Chinese version of a deck of cards. A mahjong set usually has 152 tiles, 108 of which are suit tiles (there are three suits). The rest are symbols and are generally more valuable than the suit tiles. The object of the game is to builds sets of tiles.

Mahjong, as it is played in Hong Kong, is a very lively game, with much clattering of tiles and friendly conversation. Four people are needed to play the game. The tiles are turned over and mixed up. Each player then picks a certain number of tiles. The players take turns to discard and pick up new tiles, hoping to be the first to build a complete set. There are very complicated rules governing how the sets can be built. Different types of sets command different point amounts. The game can be played with or without gambling—gambling comes in when the players agree how much each point is worth.

BOARD GAMES

In parks or in the common areas in public housing estates, there will usually be men seated on stools bending over board games. These men are playing either Chinese chess or weiqi (also known as go), games that require a great deal of strategy.

Chinese chess traces its roots back to the 8th century. Chess pieces include elephants, cavalry, infantry, and a fortress where the king and his counselors are entrenched. The two halves of the board are separated by the Yellow River. The objective of the game is to storm the opponent's fortress and capture the military commanders.

Weiqi has been around for thousands of years and is the oldest board game in China. It is played on a grid of 19 horizontal and 19 vertical lines. The pieces are 181 black and 180 white flat, round counters. The object of the game is to capture the opponent's counters and territory. Because of the high number of possible moves, weiqi is considered the most complicated board game in the world.

A horse race under way at Happy Valley.

HORSE RACING

Gambling on horse races is popular among the Hong Kong Chinese. When the races are on, many people take leave from work to attend the races at Happy Valley, hoping to strike it rich. All Hong Kong residents take note of race times and dates in order to know when to avoid the masses of traffic that head to and from the racetrack.

Horse racing is organized by the Hong Kong Jockey Club, which also operates lotteries.

FESTIVALS

THE MAJOR FESTIVALS IN HONG KONG follow the Chinese calendar. The Gregorian calendar followed in the West is a solar calendar, meaning that it is based on the movements of the sun. The ancient Chinese calendar, however, is lunar (based on the moon). The starting dates of each month vary from year to year, according to the phases of the moon.

The Lunar New Year is the most important festival in Hong Kong. Other important Chinese festivals are the Ching Ming Festival in spring, the Dragon Boat Festival in early summer, the Festival of Hungry Ghosts, and the Mid-Autumn Festival. These festivals are thousands of years old and are celebrated by Chinese all over the world.

THE CHINESE ZODIAC

The Chinese calendar moves in a 12-year cycle. Each year is dedicated to an animal. According to legend, Buddha summoned all the animals of the kingdom when he was dying. The first 12 to arrive had years assigned to them. People born under each sign are said to possess certain characteristics.

Rat (1972, 1984, 1996)   – charming, smart, creative, thrifty
Ox (1973, 1985, 1997)   – steadfast, methodical, reliable
Tiger (1974, 1986, 1998)   – dynamic, warm, sincere
Rabbit (1975, 1987, 1999)   – humble, artistic, clear-sighted
Dragon (1976, 1988, 2000)   – flamboyant, imaginative, lucky
Snake (1977, 1989, 2001)   – discreet, sensual, refined, intelligent
Horse (1978, 1990, 2002)   – sociable, competitive, adamant
Sheep (1979, 1991, 2003)   – artistic, fastidious, weak-willed
Monkey (1980, 1992, 2004)   – witty, popular, versatile, good-humored
Rooster (1981, 1993, 2005)   – aggressive, alert, a perfectionist
Dog (1982, 1994, 2006)   – honest, traditional, sympathetic
Pig (1983, 1995, 2007)   – caring, diligent, home-loving

Most businesses close during the three public holidays of the Chinese New Year, and a few close for longer. About a week before the new year, barbers and hairdressers charge double their usual prices, since almost everyone needs a haircut to look good for the new year!

Opposite: **At the Bun Festival, children can be seen "floating" in the air, dressed as characters from Chinese myths. They are supported by wires attached to harnesses under their clothing.**

Children perform a lion dance for Chinese New Year.

CHINESE NEW YEAR

The first day of the first lunar month is Chinese New Year, the most important festival for Hong Kong Chinese. It falls in late January or February. As it marks the start of the year, every care is taken to ensure good fortune for the year. Buildings are decorated and the streets are strung with elaborate light displays. A huge fireworks display is held over Victoria Harbor, usually on the second day of the new year. Lion dances and other celebrations can be seen at hotels and in residential areas.

Preparations for the new year begin with a thorough spring cleaning. The home is decorated with good luck symbols, such as bushes laden with tiny oranges (kumquats)—the Chinese word for kumquats sounds like the words for gold and lucky. People buy new clothes, fill rice bins and larders to the brim, mend quarrels, and repay debts.

On New Year's Day, everyone dresses up in new clothes to visit relatives and friends, and children receive laisee. People greet one another with "*Kung Hay Fat Choy*," meaning "wishing you prosperity." On this day, no work—not even housework—should be done, in case good luck is inadvertently chased away. Knives and scissors should not be used. Even a fall is a bad omen.

In the evening, the most important event is the reunion dinner. No matter how far they are from home, people make an effort to have dinner with their parents on New Year's Eve. Certain foods are traditional, such as raw fish, which symbolizes prosperity, and New Year's cake made from rice flour. At midnight, all the lights in the house are turned on to dispel bad luck that may be hidden in dark corners. Crowds pack the temples to offer prayers for prosperity in the new year.

In some villages of the New Territories, lanterns are hung in ancestral halls during Chinese New Year. Any local family who had a son born during the past year brings a lantern to the hall, and the men of the family gather to enjoy a special meal. It is a time of community-wide celebration.

Choosing lucky charms to decorate the house. The most auspicious colors are red and gold.

THE KITCHEN GOD'S DAY

On the day before the lunar new year, the Kitchen God judges the family's behavior and travels to heaven to make a report to the Jade Emperor. The picture of the Kitchen God is taken down and ceremonially burned outside the kitchen to send him on his way. Before he goes, he is worshiped with incense and candles and given a delicious meal of glutinous rice, honey, or sugar, and sometimes wine as well. They are smeared all over his mouth to make sure that what he says will be sweet and flattering.

HUNGRY GHOSTS

The Chinese believe that there are enormous numbers of ghosts in the world. People may become ghosts if all their descendants die out, if they die without children, or if they were unable to reach the afterworld because they did not have a proper funeral.

The seventh lunar month is a dangerous time because the gates of the underworld are opened and ghosts are free to roam wherever they like. Therefore, it is necessary to placate them by offering them gifts of food and entertaining them with opera.

During the seventh month, temporary wooden structures are built in open spaces. On one side is a stage for opera performances. The other side has an altar where huge sticks of incense are burned night and day. Worshipers come here to pray and place fresh incense sticks. Behind the altar is a temporary temple. Images of deities from the local temples are carried here in sedan chairs.

The climax of the festival is the offering of food and the burning of paper clothing and spirit money to the hungry ghosts. The food is distributed among the faithful on the last evening.

Besides the big ceremonies, many smaller ones are performed during the first two weeks of this month. Believers make their own offerings and burn paper money to the restless spirits.

On the harbor, decorated boats take offerings to ghosts who died at sea. When Buddhist monks or Taoist priests chant their liturgies on the boat, believers scatter rice upon the water and launch paper boats filled with gifts.

THE MID-AUTUMN FESTIVAL

The 15th day of the eighth lunar month is the time when the moon is at its fullest and brightest. This is the time of the Mid-Autumn Festival, one of the loveliest nights of the year. During the Mid-Autumn Festival, children walk around with lanterns and look for the lady in the moon. According to legend, Chang Er, the woman in the moon, had a husband who was a tyrant. He had a potion that would make him immortal. Fearing for her people, Chang Er drank the potion instead and flew to the moon.

Traditionally, the Mid-Autumn Festival was mainly a women's festival. A table was set up facing the moon with dishes of round foods such as apples, oranges, peaches, and mooncakes (pastries filled with sweet, mashed lotus seeds). Rice, wine, and tea were offered, together with a few suits of paper clothing and many ingots of spirit money made of gold and silver paper. Shops sell special decorations and brightly colored lanterns. Today, plastic lanterns in the shape of military tanks or Mickey Mouse are common. It has become the custom to take children to high vantage points, such as Victoria Peak, to light lanterns and enjoy the moon.

Above: **A girl waits with her lotus-shaped lantern at the Mid-Autumn Festival.**

Opposite: **Enormous decorated incense sticks are burned at the Festival of the Hungry Ghosts.**

Above: **Offerings are made to the Goddess of the Sea at the Tin Hau festival.**

Opposite: **Ching Ming combines the ritual of honoring family ancestors with an enjoyable day out for the family.**

FESTIVAL OF TIN HAU

Tin Hau, Queen of Heaven and Goddess of the Sea, has a special place in Hong Kong's heart.

Legend has it that Tin Hau was once a mortal. She was born long ago on the 23rd day of the third lunar month. Shortly before her birth, a red light was seen descending upon the house of her father, a poor fisherman.

One day, Tin Hau dreamed that she saw her father and two brothers on their fishing junks in a storm. In her dream, she grabbed the rigging and started to pull them ashore. At that moment, her mother woke Tin Hau, causing her to let go of one ropes. When her brothers returned, they said that a beautiful girl had walked across the raging waters and dragged their junk to safety but had been unable to save their father.

After Tin Hau's death, sailors began to tell stories of her appearing in stormy weather and saving them from certain death. The red light that appeared at the time of her birth was seen upon masts and greeted as a sign of her protection, called "Our Mother's Fire."

Today, almost every Hong Kong ship carries her image, and dozens of temples in Hong Kong are dedicated to her. On her birthday, fishermen decorate their boats and gather at her temples to pray for good catches during the coming year.

CHING MING

In April, on the 106th day after the winter solstice, families visit cemeteries to sweep their ancestors' graves, repaint the inscriptions on the headstones, and show their respect. This festival is called Ching Ming, meaning "Clear and Bright." Incense sticks and red candles are lit. Rice, wine, tea, and other foods are set out, and paper clothing and spirit money are burned. The whole family kneels to pay their respects. Before they leave, they tuck several pieces of offering paper under a stone on top of the grave. This is a sign that the grave has been tended for another year.

Despite its solemn origins, Ching Ming rites have the atmosphere of a picnic because the food offerings are eaten by the family members. It is a happy occasion when families get together to remember their ancestors.

THE BUN FESTIVAL

Unique to Hong Kong, the Bun Festival takes place on Cheung Chau. The central attraction is three 60-foot (18-m) towers studded with pink and white buns. The buns are an offering to the ghosts of islanders who, according to alternative stories, were killed by a plague or by pirates.

During the four days of the celebration there are religious observances, processions, and Chinese opera performances. On the third day, people dressed in colorful costumes march, walk on stilts, or ride on floats through the winding streets of the village. At the end of the festival, after the ghosts have had their fill, the buns are distributed to the crowds.

A lion dance at the Bun Festival, with the towers of buns behind. At the climax of the festival, the crowds used to scramble up the towers to claim buns for good luck. After fights broke out and a tower collapsed, the scramble was abandoned.

THE DRAGON BOAT FESTIVAL

The Dragon Boat Festival, celebrated in the fifth lunar month, combines a traditional celebration with an exciting, fast-paced sporting event.

The tradition originated with the story of Wat Yuen, a famous poet and royal minister who threw himself into a river when his king refused to heed his wise advice. When the people realized that Wat Yuen was drowned, they threw rice into the water in the hope that the fish would eat the rice and spare his body. The dragon boats race every year as if they are looking for Wat Yuen, and everybody eats sticky rice wrapped up in leaves.

The dragon boat rowers sit two abreast in the long, narrow body of the dragon. The heads and tails are dismantled and kept in local temples when not in use. New heads must be dedicated in a ceremony that involves painting each eye with a dot of vermilion paint mixed with blood from the comb of a brown chicken. Once this is done, the dragon is "alive" and has to be treated with respect, presented with candles and incense, and protected from anything that might harm it.

Rowers paddle furiously in a dragon boat race in Hong Kong. Dragon Boat Festivals have become increasingly popular among non-Chinese in other parts of the world. Since 1991, there has been an annual dragon boat race in New York, which attracts partici-pants from all over the world.

TA CHIU

In addition to lesser gods and ghosts, Taoists believe in three great spirits—the Three Pure Ones. These pure spirits live in the stars, at the true source of life, beyond the reach of change or decay.

The aim of Ta Chiu is to invite the Three Pure Ones down so that they will wipe away evil, restore peace and harmony, and renew life for the entire population of a sizable group of villages. Ordinary villagers leave the rituals to the Taoist priests. They are content to make offerings to their own patron gods, renounce evil, do good deeds, and feed the hungry ghosts.

Taoist priests perform Ta Chiu rituals to bless a village.

The Ta Chiu ceremonies are carried out on several levels. Taoist priests perform a ceremony for the Three Pure Ones in the temple. Operas are performed, and offerings are brought to the patron deities, whose images have been brought out of the temple and put in a temporary shrine for the occasion. Birds and fish are liberated as a symbolic giving of life. Purification is carried out by cleansing the altar, ritual bathing, fasting, and disposing of unclean things, which the priests collect and burn in a large paper boat.

Finally, there are two spectacular closing ceremonies. The priests read out the names of all the villagers from a huge list. After that, they send the list to heaven in flames on the back of a paper horse, and then post a red paper duplicate list on the wall for all to see. At midnight on the last night, they preside over an enormous "clothes burning" at which ghosts are fed, clothed, given money, and sent away. All the villagers eat a communal meal at which the meat of the "golden pigs"—part of the offering to the gods—is the most honored dish.

PUBLIC HOLIDAYS

Hong Kong has 17 public holidays. Among these are New Year's Day (January 1), Easter (March or April), Ching Ming (April), Dragon Boat Festival (June), Mid-Autumn Festival (September), and Christmas Day (December 25). Chinese New Year is a three-day public holiday in January or February.

Some public holidays have changed since Hong Kong became a Special Administrative Region of China. Festivals with a British focus have been eliminated, and new festivals have been introduced. For example, the Queen's birthday, which used to be marked with two public holidays in June, is no longer celebrated. Liberation Day, in August, used to commemorate the Allied liberation of Hong Kong during World War II; it now commemorates victory in the Second Sino-Japanese War. New holidays include June 1 and 2, which commemorate the change of sovereignty, and October 1 and 2, which celebrate China's National Day.

A colorful display of Christmas lights. Hong Kong's Christian, Hindu, Jewish, and Sikh communities celebrate their own festivals.

FOOD

HONG KONG'S SOPHISTICATED food culture reflects the richness of China's culinary arts. Chinese cuisine is probably the aspect of Chinese culture that foreigners know best. Chinese restaurants can be found in almost every country. It's said that the Chinese are lucky people—wherever they go, they can always have hometown food! Much of the Chinese food available in Europe and North America is a variation of Cantonese cuisine, having been introduced by immigrants from Hong Kong.

A typical Hong Kong meal begins with tea. An appetizer, such as cold cuts of meat, follows. The main dishes come next. There could be as many as 10 courses for a formal dinner such as a wedding banquet. For a more ordinary family meal, there are may be three or four dishes of meat and vegetables plus a soup, followed by dessert.

An old Chinese saying indicates how highly the cuisine of the Guangzhou (Canton) area is regarded: "To be born in Suzhou, to live in Hangzhou, to eat in Guangzhou, and to die in Liuzhou."

Left: **Fresh vegetables are an important part of Cantonese cuisine.**

Opposite: **A selection of dried meats, including pork sausages, fish, and flattened ducks, at a market stall.**

Food is cooked quickly in a wok at a high heat.

CANTONESE CUISINE

As most Hong Kong Chinese originated in the area around Guangzhou (Canton), Cantonese cuisine is by far the most popular cuisine in Hong Kong. This is the cuisine that most people abroad know as Chinese food. Part of the reason Cantonese cuisine is so popular is its method of preparation. Food is cooked quickly and lightly in a little water or oil, usually in a wok. This seals in and preserves the flavors of the food.

Cantonese cuisine is known for its fresh, delicate flavors. Fresh ingredients are prepared the same day and cooked just before serving. Seafood is so fresh it hardly touches dry land before it arrives on your dinner table—in many seafood restaurants, you can actually choose your own fish from the tanks in which they are swimming. Frozen and processed foods are not usually found in Chinese kitchens. However, dried seafoods, such as shark's fin and abalone, are often used.

Many dishes, especially vegetables and fish, are steamed. This avoids overcooking and preserves the delicate flavors of the food. The use of hot and spicy sauces is not common in Cantonese cuisine. Sauces are used to enhance flavors, not overpower them. They usually contain ingredients with contrasting flavors, such as vinegar and sugar or ginger and onion.

Barbecued meats, especially *char siu* ("chah syoo," sweet barbecued pork) and *siu ngor* ("syoo or," barbecued goose), shark's fin soup, crabs steamed or cooked in black bean sauce, congee (thick Cantonese rice porridge), and the ubiquitous dim sum are some of the better-known Cantonese dishes.

DIM SUM

Dim sum, a special Cantonese snack, is served in many Cantonese restaurants in Hong Kong. This branch of Cantonese cuisine dates from the 10th century. Dim sum literally means "to touch the heart." Dim sum are bite-sized morsels of food, such as steamed or fried dumplings filled with meat or seafood, Chinese buns stuffed with sweet bean paste, spring rolls, chicken's feet, rice wrapped in leaves, and stuffed bean curd.

Dim sum forms part of the Chinese tradition of *yum cha* (Cantonese for "drinking tea"). Dim sum originated from the need to eat something during yum cha, when friends and colleagues would get together to discuss everything from business to family gossip. At a yum cha restaurant, the guests drink tea and choose dishes of dim sum from trays that are wheeled around the restaurant.

There's an interesting tradition associated with yum cha. When people receive tea, they tap the table twice with the knuckles of two fingers, instead of saying "thank you." Legend has it that a Chinese emperor went south disguised as an ordinary citizen, accompanied by his bodyguards. One day in a teahouse, the emperor himself poured the tea for one of his bodyguards. Instead of kneeling and bowing, which would have given away his emperor's identity, the bodyguard knocked on the table with two knuckles, so that his fingers resembled kneeling legs. This gesture of respect gave rise to a tradition that is still practiced today.

YIN AND YANG FOODS

The Chinese believe that all foods fall into three basic categories. Yang (or "heaty") food heats the blood and reduces vital energy. Yin (or "cooling") foods cool the blood and increase vital energy. Neutral foods are balanced and do not effect energy. Fried foods, lamb, mutton, chocolate, almonds, mangoes, and potato chips are examples of yang foods. Melons, apples, yogurt, pork, celery, salt, and bananas are all yin foods.

Winter is the time for yang foods, when the blood needs to be heated, and summer is the time for yin food. When ordering food in restaurants, the Hong Kong Chinese try to maintain a balance between yin and yang foods. Fried yang food may be teamed with steamed yin dishes, and heaty meat dishes are teamed with cooling vegetable dishes.

DRINKS

Common non-alcoholic drinks in Hong Kong include soft drinks, many varieties of Chinese tea, and local specialties such as soya bean drinks.

Some Chinese drink Western wine, but it is more common to see local beer and spirits on the dining table. Chinese wine is often rice-based and distilled. Cognac is a popular drink, especially for entertaining favored guests. Like the exotic dishes served in restaurants, its cost is designed to impress. Brands like Remy Martin and Courvoisier are consumed like water. Hong Kong is the world's highest per capita consumer of cognac.

Fish and shellfish are traded at the fish market at Aberdeen.

EXOTIC FOODS

The Cantonese are well-known for what some consider their bizarre taste in meat. The Hong Kong Chinese are no exception. The Chinese believe that the more exotic the meat, the more salubrious its effects on their health. Snake is boiled into a thick soup. Frog's legs fried with ginger and scallions are thought to strengthen one's legs. Bird's nest soup is made from the dried mucus of the swallow's salivary gland, which it uses to line its nest. Shark's fins are made into soup. Sea slugs, crocodiles, and sundry other creatures are prepared in a variety of ways. Some Chinese delicacies, such as bear's paws, are banned in Hong Kong.

These rice wines contain baby rats and a snake. The Chinese believe they have curative powers.

BEEF IN BLACK BEAN SAUCE

(Serves four)

Marinade
- 1 tablespoon Chinese rice wine or dry sherry
- 1 teaspoon salt

Seasonings
- 2 tablespoons beef stock
- $1\frac{1}{2}$ tablespoons black bean garlic sauce
- 1 tablespoon soy sauce
- 1 tablespoon crushed garlic

$\frac{3}{4}$ pound (340g) beef steak, cut into thin strips
$2\frac{1}{2}$ tablespoons cooking oil
$\frac{1}{2}$ onion, cut into 1-inch (2.5-cm) squares
$\frac{1}{2}$ small green bell pepper, cut into 1-inch (2.5-cm) squares
$\frac{1}{2}$ small red bell pepper, cut into 1-inch (2.5-cm) squares
1 teaspoon cornstarch, dissolved in 2 teaspoons water

Combine marinade ingredients and beef in a bowl. Stir until the beef is coated. Let stand for 10 minutes. Combine seasoning ingredients in a bowl; set aside.

Place a wok over high heat until hot. Add 2 tablespoons oil, swirling to coat sides. Add marinated beef and stir-fry for 2 minutes. Remove beef from wok and set aside.

Heat remaining $\frac{1}{2}$ tablespoon oil in wok, swirling to coat sides. Add onion and bell peppers; stir-fry for 1 minute. Return beef to wok and add seasonings; bring to a boil. Add cornstarch solution and cook, stirring, until sauce boils and thickens. Serve hot with steamed rice.

TABLE ETIQUETTE

There is a strict etiquette for eating with chopsticks. Chopsticks should never be used to drum on the table, and it is most disrespectful to point them at another person or use them to gesture. When not in use, chopsticks should be placed flat, not left standing vertically in a bowl but should be laid flat. Sometimes, for the sake of hygiene, diners will turn their chopsticks around and use the reverse end to take food from the serving dishes.

At mealtimes, whether at home or in a restaurant, it is customary to wait for everyone to be seated before beginning the meal. Children generally invite their elders to begin before helping themselves.

Large Chinese dining tables in Hong Kong usually have a rotating platform called a lazy susan in the center, on which the dishes are placed. Diners help themselves to a morsel of the dish in front of them, and then rotate the lazy susan, helping themselves to each dish along the way. Food should be taken from the top of the plate. It is considered rude to dig around for a morsel of food. The choice morsels should also be avoided—they should be offered to the elders at the table or to honored guests. A good host will always tend to his or her guests and urge them to eat more.

The Chinese do not pour soy sauce on their rice, as this would swamp the subtle flavors of the meal. Instead, the sauce is placed in a small side dish.

Hong Kongers do not linger at the table. When the last course has been served and eaten, the meal is over.

At a Chinese meal, communal dishes are placed at the center of the table, and everyone helps themselves. It's a very sociable way to enjoy a meal.

HONG KONG

CHINA
(Guangdong Province)

Deep Bay

Sham Chun River

● Fanling

Starling Inlet

Mai Po Marshes

Yuen Long ●

● Tai Po

Tolo Harbor

Zhu Jiang River Delta

NEW TERRITORIES

Tuen Mun ●

Tai Mo Shan ▲
(3,140ft/957m)

Sha Tin ●

Ma On Shan ▲

High Island

Tsuen Wan ●

Kwai Chung ●

Tsing Yi Island

Tate Cairn ▲

Ho Chung ●

Port Shelter (Ngau Mei Hoi)

NEW KOWLOON

▲ *Kowloon Peak*

Stonecutters Island

KOWLOON

Kowloon Bay

Kwun Tong ●

Tsim Sha Tsui ●

Junk Bay

Clear Water Bay

Chek Lap Kok

Central District (Victoria) ●

Victoria Harbor

● Wanchai

Lantau Island (Tai Yue Shan)

Victoria Peak ▲

● Happy Valley

Cape Collinson

Joss House Bay

Tai O ●

▲ *Sunset Peak*

Telegraph Bay

Hong Kong Island

Mt. Parker ▲

▲ *Lantau Peak*

Wah Fu ●

● Aberdeen

● Shek O

Deep Water Bay

Stanley ●

Repulse Bay

Tai Tam Bay

Lamma Island

Stanley Bay

Cheung Chau

SOUTH CHINA SEA

N

●	Capital city
●	Major town
▲	Mountain peak

Feet		Meters
16,500		5,000
9,900		3,000
6,600		2,000
3,300		1,000
1,650		500
660		200
0		0

0	2	4	6	8	10 Miles
0		5	10	15 Kilometers	

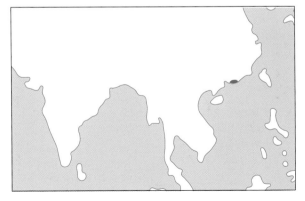

QUICK NOTES

OFFICIAL STATUS
Special Administrative Region of the People's Republic of China

LAND AREA
412 square miles (1,067 square km)

POPULATION
6.3 million

POPULATION DENSITY
15,000 per square mile (5,790 per square km)

LIFE EXPECTANCY
75.4 years (men), 81 years (women)

MAJOR RIVER
Sham Chun River

HIGHEST POINT
Tai Mo Shan, 3,140 feet (957 m)

AVERAGE ANNUAL RAINFALL
85 inches (2.16 m)

OFFICIAL LANGUAGES
English and Chinese

MAJOR RELIGIONS
Buddhism and Taoism

SYMBOL
The Bauhinia flower

CURRENCY
Hong Kong dollar
US$1 = HK$7.80

MAIN EXPORTS
Garments and fabrics, electronic goods

MAIN IMPORTS
Machinery and transportation equipment, textiles, chemicals, electronic goods, food and livestock

IMPORTANT HISTORICAL DATES
1839–42—First Opium War. China cedes Hong Kong Island to Britain.
1856–60—Second Opium War. China cedes Kowloon to Britain.
July 1, 1898—China leases New Territories to Britain for 99 years.
1937–1945—Sino-Japanese War.
1941–45—Japanese occupation of Hong Kong
May 1967—Labor riots in Hong Kong.
1982—China and Britain begin formal negotiations over Hong Kong.
December 19, 1984—Signing of the Sino-British Joint Declaration.
April 4, 1990—Basic Law adopted.
July 1, 1997—Hong Kong returns to Chinese rule as a Special Administrative Region.

LEADING PERSONALITIES
Tung Chee Hwa, Chief Executive of Hong Kong
Christopher Patten, last British governor of Hong Kong
Lee Lai Shan, Hong Kong's only Olympic medallist
Jacky Cheung, Leon Lai, Andy Lau, Anita Mui, Faye Wong—popular singers
Jackie Chan, Maggie Cheung, Chow Yuen Fat, Bruce Lee, Jet Li—popular actors
John Woo, film director

GLOSSARY

char siu ("chah syoo")
Sweet barbecued pork.

chi ("chee")
Spirit, energy.

congee ("con-gee")
The English name for Cantonese rice porridge ("juk" in Cantonese).

dim sum
Dumplings or other foods eaten in small portions, particularly while drinking tea.

fung shui ("fung soy")
An ancient system of attaining good health and fortune through a harmonious environment.

gweilo ("gwy-loh")
Caucasian person (literally "foreign devil").

laisee ("ly-see")
Red packets of lucky money given at Chinese New Year and other special occasions.

laissez faire ("LESS-ay FAIR")
The practice of non-interference in the affairs of others. Often used to describe a government with minimal involvement in economic affairs.

joss stick
Incense stick ("joss" means "luck").

junk
A Chinese sailing ship.

karaoke ("ka-ra-OH-kay")
Singing along to prerecorded instrumental music.

mahjong ("mah-jong")
A Chinese game of tiles played by four people.

mooncakes
Pastries filled with sweet lotus paste.

siu ngor ("syoo or")
Barbecued goose.

spirit money
Pretend paper money that is burned as an offering to gods or ancestral ghosts.

tai chi ("ty chee")
A Chinese martial art charcterized by meditative exercises.

tao ("tow", rhymes with "now")
In the Taoist religion, the spiritual path that leads to immortality.

weiqi ("way-chee")
A Chinese board game.

yang
Energy that is positive and active.

yin
Energy that is negative and passive.

yum cha
To drink tea.

zham cha ("tsum chah")
To serve tea.

zhang ("tsang")
Cool, neat, excellent.

BIBLIOGRAPHY

Fyson, Nance Lui. *Hong Kong (World in View)*. Steck-Vaughn: Austin, 1990.

Miller, John, and Kirsten Miller (editors). *Hong Kong (Chronicles Abroad)*. Chronicle Books: San Fransisco, 1994.

Thomas, Ted, and Nicole Turner. *What's Going to Happen in 1997 in Hong Kong?* Simon and Schuster (Asia): Singapore, 1996.

Wei, Betty, and Elizabeth Li. *Culture Shock! Hong Kong*. Graphic Arts Center: Portland, 1995.

Wiltshire, Trea. *Old Hong Kong*. Weatherhill: New York, 1994.

Yahuda, Michael. *Hong Kong: China's Challenge*. Routledge: New York, 1996.

INDEX

INDEX

INDEX

PICTURE CREDITS

J
951.25   Kagda, Falaq.
K   Hong Kong.

DISCARD